Research and Development

With Patent Box

2nd Edition

James Boughton

Disclaimer

Claritax Books is a trading name of Claritax Books Ltd.

Claritax Books Ltd
6 Grosvenor Park Road
Chester
CH1 1QQ

Company number 07658388
VAT number 114 9371 20

Law date

The text is based on the tax law as at 1 April 2019.

First edition December 2014
This edition April 2019

Research and Development

With Patent Box

2nd Edition

James Boughton

Published by:

Claritax Books Ltd
6 Grosvenor Park Road
Chester, CH1 1QQ

www.claritaxbooks.com

ISBN: 978-1-908545-75-6

Other titles from Claritax Books

Other titles from Claritax Books include:

- A-Z of Plant & Machinery
- Advising British Expats
- Capital Allowances
- Construction Industry Scheme
- Discovery Assessments
- Employee Benefits & Expenses
- Employee Share Schemes
- Employment Status
- Enterprise Investment Scheme
- Financial Planning with Trusts
- Furnished Holiday Lettings
- Main Residence Relief
- Managing Risk
- Pension Tax Guide
- Personal Representatives
- Residence: The Definition in Practice
- Stamp Duty Land Tax
- Tax Chamber Hearings
- Tax Losses
- VAT Registration

See www.claritaxbooks.com for details of further titles due for publication in the coming months.

About the author

James Boughton CTA

James Boughton is a senior tax manager with Mazars and works extensively in the field of research and development tax reliefs and the Patent Box.

Mazars is an international accounting firm with a UK business ranking in the top 10 UK accounting firms by fee income. Mazars has a large tax advisory practice, including a core team of R&D tax specialists.

James may be contacted by email at james.boughton@mazars.co.uk.

Acknowledgements

I would like to thank Lindsay Pentelow and Sam Boughton for their encouragement and support in relation to the original version of this book, and Colin Copeland for his guidance and practical help in preparing this second edition.

Abbreviations

BIS	(Department for) Business, Innovation and Skills
CIRD	Corporate Intangibles and Research & Development manual
CSA	Cost sharing arrangement
CTA	Corporation Tax Act
DTI	Department of Trade and Industry
EEA	European Economic Area
EPW	Externally provided workers
FA	Finance Act
FRS	Financial Reporting Standards
GAAP	Generally Accepted Accounting Principles
Guidelines	Guidelines of the Dept. for Business, Innovation and Skills
HMRC	HM Revenue & Customs
IAS	International Accounting Standards
IFRS	International Financial Reporting Standards
IP	Intellectual property
IPR	(Special) IP rate (of corporation tax)
ITA	Income Tax Act
LLP	Limited liability partnership
MR	Main rate (of corporation tax)
NI(C)	National Insurance (contributions)
NSA	Notified state aid
OECD	Organisation for Economic Co-operation and Development
QRP	Qualifying residual profit
R&D	Research and development
RDAs	Research and development allowances
RDEC	R&D expenditure credit
RIPI	Relevant IP income
RP	Relevant IP profits
SC	Staff controller
SI	Specified investor
SME	Small or medium-sized enterprise
SP	Staff provider
SSAP	Statement of Standard Accounting Practice
STA	Scientific or technological advance
STU	Scientific or technological uncertainty
TI	Total income
UKGAAP	Generally Accepted Accounting Practice in the UK
VC	Venture capital

Table of contents

Introduction

The system of tax relief for research and development (R&D) and intellectual property ownership is a key part of the UK's incentives for innovation and is important in making the UK an attractive place for innovative companies to do business.

As set out by David Gauke, Financial Secretary, in October 2015:

> "Research and Development (R&D) is crucial for an economy's productivity and long-run growth. This is why R&D tax relief plays a key role in the government's objective for productive investment."[1]

As the R&D tax relief has been around for 18 years a question that may arise is whether it is really worth considering now if a claim has not already been made. There are four key reasons why a claim may be appropriate.

- Firstly, the relief can lead to cash repayments from HMRC; cash is always essential to the success of a business. In the uncertain economic environment we find ourselves in, this is so more than ever.
- Secondly, the relief has been improved considerably over the years. The rate of the relief has more than doubled for some since its introduction.
- Thirdly, certain conditions have been removed altogether over the years and so a claim which was not possible previously may be possible now. Companies that have looked at the relief in the past and decided against claiming should take another look.
- Finally, the relief is generally underutilised with many eligible companies not claiming. Where a competitor is claiming relief but the business in question is not, the business is placing itself at a competitive disadvantage as, in effect, its real costs of undertaking R&D are higher.

[1] HMRC (October 2015) Making R&D Easier – HMRC's plan for small business R&D tax relief

Since 1 April 2013, certain income derived from patents has been eligible for a reduced rate of corporation tax through the Patent Box. Potentially, the relief reduces the corporate tax rate on patent-related income to 10%.

The Patent Box is designed to work alongside the R&D tax reliefs to incentivise companies to keep their intellectual property in the UK after it is developed. There are specific rules which "carve out" the benefit from the R&D relief when calculating the Patent Box relief. This means that the benefit of the Patent Box is not reduced by a claim for R&D relief, and vice versa. The powerful combination of the R&D relief and the Patent Box can give cash back during the development phase and then provide a low tax rate once the company is making a profit.

This book is designed to be a practical guide to the R&D tax relief and Patent Box rules. It is written to help entrepreneurs to take advantage of this relief to save cash, which can then be used to fuel further innovation.

The 2016 United Kingdom European Union membership referendum and Brexit have placed doubt in the mind of some about the future of the R&D tax relief. It appears that relief remains at the centre of the plans to make the UK an attractive place to undertake R&D. This was reinforced in a speech to the Confederation of British Industry in 2016 on "Brexit" given by the Prime Minister, Theresa May. When speaking of the relief given by the R&D credit she stated:

> "Now we want to go further, and look at how we can make our support even more effective – because my aim is not simply for the UK to have the lowest corporate tax rate in the G20, but also a tax system that is profoundly pro-innovation."

(https://www.gov.uk/government/speeches/cbi-annual-conference-2016-prime-ministers-speech.)

The law referred to in this book is as stated on the inner front cover, but tax rules constantly evolve.

1. First principles

1.1 Who should consider a claim?

The first question to be addressed is whether a claim can be made. The short answer is that a company should consider a claim if it is creating a product or process which is an improvement on what is already available and which involves the use of science or technology. There are many further hurdles to overcome but this is the core around which the claim can be constructed.

1.2 Benefits

If there is a chance of a claim, the next step will be to ascertain what the benefits would be. The amount of the relief will depend on various factors which are discussed in more detail later.

Relief is primarily given as a "super-deduction" in the claimant company's corporation tax return. This means that tax relief for "qualifying expenditure" is enhanced. This in turn reduces the company's taxable profits and consequently the company's corporation tax liability. The current rate of super-deduction is 230% which means that for every £100,000 the company spends on qualifying R&D expenditure it reduces its corporation tax profits by £230,000. At a corporation tax rate of 19% (from 1 April 2017) a company spending £100,000 on a new development will have its corporation tax liability reduced by £43,700 in total (£230,000 x 19%), of which £24,700 has been as a result of the R&D claim. This means that just under half of the cost of the development has been met by tax relief.

There is an additional option for relief where a company is making a tax loss. In this case, since the company is not paying any corporation tax, it would not be able to get immediate relief from a super-deduction. The relief is extended in these cases so that a company can claim a tax credit of up to just over a third of the qualifying costs. This can be very important to companies in the development phase of their products and creates an additional source of project finance.

These are the most beneficial rates of relief, and are only available to small or medium-sized enterprises ("SMEs").

On 1 April 2013 the most ground-breaking changes to the R&D expenditure reliefs since the introduction of the "large super-deduction scheme" in 2002 came into effect. Since this date large enterprises and SMEs claiming under the large scheme for SMEs have been able to claim an R&D expenditure credit ("RDEC"). The credit is treated as income in the accounts of the company and is included in the profit before tax, which is why it was originally referred to as the "above the line credit". The RDEC is included as income within the profit and loss account of the company in a similar way to a grant and the income is then taxed in the same way as other income of the company.

The current headline rate of the RDEC is 12% (for expenditure incurred on or after 1 January 2018). At a tax rate of 19% this gives a cash benefit of £9,720 if a large enterprise spends £100,000 on R&D (9.72% of the qualifying spend). A key benefit of the RDEC scheme over its predecessor is that it gives the option for cash repayment where the company is not paying corporation tax. The change of mechanism brought about by the introduction of the RDEC did not change the underlying qualification and the categories of qualifying expenditure. The RDEC is covered in more detail in **Chapter 6**.

For expenditure up to 31 March 2016 it was possible to claim under the old "super-deduction" scheme. The rate available to larger companies was lower than for SMEs, i.e. 130% rather than 230%. This means that if a large enterprise spends £100,000 on qualifying R&D it will get total tax relief of £24,700, of which £5,700 would be as a result of the R&D claim (using 19% for comparison purposes). The cash benefit of this relief was lower than relief under the RDEC scheme so a claim under the RDEC scheme is generally more beneficial during the period the schemes ran concurrently. Although theoretically claims could be made under the super-deduction scheme for large companies, this is not covered in detail in this book due to the higher benefit of the RDEC scheme.

1.3 Mechanism for making a claim

R&D tax reliefs are claimed through the corporation tax return (CT600) of a company. This can be done in an original return or through an amendment to a filed return. In this way, it is possible to claim for more than one year at a time, especially where no claim has been made in the past. A CT600 can typically be amended within two years of the end of the accounting period. More detail on this subject is included in **Chapter 8**.

Example

Alpha Ltd manufactures plastic packaging and has made considerable improvements to its manufacturing process. It has a 31 March year end and has spent £100,000 per year for the three years to 31 March 2019 on employing staff to undertake development related to the improvements. Alpha Ltd has been successful over recent years and has paid tax at the full rate in each year.

A claim in relation to this expenditure gives rise to a cash saving of £75,400 over the three years.

Year ended 31 March 2017

Additional tax relief	£130,000
Cash repayment	£ 26,000 (20% tax rate)

Year ended 31 March 2018

Additional tax relief	£130,000
Cash repayment	£24,700 (19% tax rate)

Year ended 31 Mach 2019

Additional tax relief	£130,000
Cash repayment	£24,700 (19% tax rate)

If (for example) the company finds out in December 2018 that it is eligible to claim, it may make a claim at that time for the earlier two years together.

1.4 Different schemes

As mentioned above, the benefit from the scheme initially depends on the size of the company.

It is also possible for SME companies that are barred from claiming under the SME scheme to claim a modified version of the RDEC scheme. This is possible where a company is prevented from claiming under the SME scheme because:

- the expenditure is subsidised by another party ("subsidised SME") (see **7.3**);
- the R&D work is subcontracted to the SME ("subcontracted SME") (see **7.2**); or
- the R&D relief under the SME has been capped ("capped SME") (see **7.4**).

The SME scheme offers a higher rate of relief (currently over two and a half times more benefit than the RDEC scheme) and should allow relief for more expenditure, especially as work that is subcontracted out to other companies can qualify.

1.5 Interaction with Patent Box

The Patent Box was introduced on 1 April 2013 for companies exploiting intellectual property in the form of patent rights (and certain other eligible rights).

The R&D tax relief benefits companies both when they are making profits (through the super-deduction) and also if they are loss making (through the repayable credit) – for example during the development phase.

The Patent Box is a relief which can reduce the tax rate to 10% and therefore primarily benefits companies that are actually paying tax – for example those that have completed the development phase and have obtained a patent to protect the valuable intellectual property which resulted from their development work.

The original consultation on the Patent Box[1] stated that:

> "The aim is to provide an additional incentive for companies in the UK to retain and commercialise existing patents and to develop new innovative patented products. This will encourage companies to locate the high-value jobs associated

1 HMRC & HM Treasury (June 2011) *Consultation on the Patent Box*

> with the development, manufacture and exploitation of patents in the UK and maintain the UK's position as a world leader in patented technologies."

Profits which qualify under the Patent Box rules can be taxed at 10%, which means that companies can almost halve their corporation tax liability on patent-related profits. Whilst the idea of the R&D reliefs is to encourage companies to develop new technologies, the idea of the Patent Box is to incentivise companies to keep their intellectual property within the UK after it has been developed.

The Patent Box rules were developed to work alongside the R&D tax credit as a package of benefits for innovative companies. Patent box ensures that the benefit of the R&D relief is maintained so the two regimes work together to ensure that companies can get tax back in the development phase and enjoy low tax rates when profits start to be made on the products or services which are developed.

The Patent Box rules were radically changed in response to the views of certain states of the European Union that the relief represented harmful tax competition. It was amended for accounting periods beginning on or after 1 July 2016 in response to recommendations from the Organisation for Economic Co-operation and Development ("OECD"). The changes included the introduction of an R&D fraction which reduces the value of the relief for intellectual property which is acquired or where the R&D relating to the intellectual property is subcontracted to connected parties.

1.6 R&D capital allowances

Capital assets cannot qualify for the R&D tax credit. There is a wealth of case law on the meaning of capital expenditure but, in summary, capital expenditure is money spent on assets which have an enduring benefit in the business. Typical examples include computers, servers, laboratory equipment and buildings (where these are not the trading stock of the business in question).

In such cases, relief may instead be claimed by way of Research & Development Allowances ("RDAs"). Generally, companies may obtain tax relief for expenditure on tangible capital assets through plant and machinery capital allowances, whereby the tax relief is typically spread over a period of time. RDAs, however, allow relief for the full cost of assets in the first year.

RDAs are considered in detail in **Chapter 9**.

2. Definition of R&D for tax purposes

2.1 Introduction

To qualify for the relief, the work which is being undertaken must be research and development within the specific definition of R&D for tax purposes. The current definition was originally issued by the then Department for Trade and Industry on 5 March 2004, and was updated on 6 December 2010. In this book, the guidelines are referred to as the "BEIS guidelines" (or just the "Guidelines") as they are now under the authority of the Department for Business, Energy and Industrial Strategy.

The Guidelines (reproduced as **Appendix 1**) run to 12 pages of detailed analysis, though in practice the question of whether work is R&D for tax purposes need not be complex or time consuming if a business is properly advised. The key point is that the benchmark is not as high as it is often believed to be. This apparent complexity of the definition is one of the reasons why more companies do not claim R&D credits.

It should be noted that the definition of R&D specifically excludes "oil and gas exploration".

Law: ITA 2007, s. 1006; CTA 2009, s. 1041; CTA 2010, s. 1138

2.2 Process

Two questions have to be answered in looking at the definition:

1. Could the activities be treated as R&D under Generally Accepted Accounting Principles ("GAAP") (the "accounts definition")?
2. Do the activities meet the definition of R&D for tax purposes (the "tax definition")?

The work must pass through these two "gateways" to be treated as R&D. But where the two definitions differ, the tax definition should take precedence. This process was considered in the case of *BE Studios Ltd v Smith & Williamson Ltd.*

Case: *BE Studios Ltd v Smith & Williamson Ltd* [2006] STC 358

2.3 The accounts definition

The first step in deciding whether an activity is R&D is to look at whether it could be treated as R&D for accounts purposes. This does not necessarily mean that it was treated as R&D in the company's accounts, only that it could have been as it is within the accounting definitions. The fact that the accounts do not reflect the R&D activity which a company is undertaking does not prevent the company from making a claim.

2.3.1 What is GAAP?

For these purposes GAAP means:

- UK GAAP, which is now set out in FRS 101 or FRS 102; or
- International Financial Reporting Standards (IFRS).

UK GAAP has undergone a process of change which is being put into effect by FRS 100, FRS 101 or FRS 102. Generally these new accounting standards came into force from 1 January 2015. The new standards move UK GAAP generally closer to IFRS and the new definition is the same as the current IFRS definition. There is no longer a separate framework for smaller entities. Certain elements of the standards do not apply to all companies, with smaller entities exempted from certain aspects. Under the new framework the definition of research and development is applicable to all entities regardless of size.

The definition under UK GAAP since moving to FRS102 has moved in line with IAS. For completeness, the definitions and guidance under both are included below.

Law: CTA 2010, s. 1127

2.3.2 UK GAAP: definition and guidance

Research is defined in the glossary of FRS 102 as:

> "Original and planned investigation undertaken with the prospect of gaining new scientific or technical knowledge and understanding."

Further, development is defined in the glossary of FRS 102 as:

> "The application of research findings or other knowledge to a plan or design for the production of new or substantially

improved materials, devices, products, processes, systems or services before the start of commercial production or use."

Examples of research are given as follows (FRS 102 18G):

"(a) Activities aimed at obtaining new knowledge.
(b) The search for, evaluation and final selection of, applications of research findings and other knowledge.
(c) The search for alternatives for materials, devices, products, processes, systems or services.
(d) The formulation, design, evaluation and final selection of possible alternatives for new or improved material, devices, projects, processes, systems or services."

Examples of development are given as follows (FRS 102 18.8J):

"(a) The design, construction and testing of pre-production or pre-use prototypes and models.
(b) The design of tools, jigs, moulds and dies involving new technology.
(c) The design, construction and operation of a pilot plant that is not of a scale economically feasible for commercial production.
(d) The design, construction and testing of a chosen alternative for new or improved materials, devices, products, processes, systems or services."

FRS 101

FRS101 is a reduced reporting framework which uses IFRS definitions as their basis. Further discussion on the IFRS definition is found at **2.3.3** immediately below.

2.3.3 IFRS definition and guidance

IFRS gives the following definitions of research and development (IAS 38):

"Research is original and planned investigation undertaken with the prospect of gaining new scientific or technical knowledge and understanding."

"Development is the application of research findings or other knowledge to a plan or design for the production of new or substantially improved materials, devices, products, processes, systems or services before the start of commercial production or use."

The standard gives the following examples of research and development activities:

Research

"• activities aimed at obtaining new knowledge;

- the search for, evaluation and final selection of, applications of research findings or other knowledge;
- the search for alternatives for materials, devices, products, processes, systems or services; and
- the formulation, design, evaluation and final selection of possible alternatives for new or improved materials, devices, products, processes, systems or services."

Development

"• the design, construction and testing of pre-production or pre-use prototypes and models;

- the design of tools, jigs, moulds and dies involving new technology;
- the design, construction and operation of a pilot plant that is not of a scale economically feasible for commercial production; and
- the design, construction and testing of a chosen alternative for new or improved materials, devices, products, processes, systems or services."

2.4 The tax definition

2.4.1 BEIS guidelines

The definition of R&D given in the "BEIS guidelines" (see the start of this chapter) is complex and runs to 12 pages. However, there are two key elements:

- scientific or technological advance; and
- scientific or technological uncertainty.

These will be dealt with in detail below.

The BEIS guidelines are referred to in this book as "the Guidelines". They are reproduced at **Appendix 1**.

Guidance: BEIS guidelines

2.4.2 Scientific or technological advance

The term "scientific or technological advance" ("STA") is defined (at para. 6 of the Guidelines) as "an advance in overall knowledge or capability in a field of science or technology".

This would appear at first glance to be a very high benchmark to meet. However, to understand how these criteria are applied in practice it is essential to look further into the guidance.

The "advance" can give rise to tangible or physical improvements, such as the development of new material, but it could also give rise to intangible advances. This could mean, for example, the development of new knowledge leading to process improvements which create cost savings.

The advance can take different forms and the following examples of advances are given in the Guidelines (at para. 9). An advance is to:

"(a) extend overall knowledge or capability in a field of science or technology; or

(b) create a process, material, device, product or service which incorporates or represents an increase in overall knowledge or capability in a field of science or technology; or

(c) make an appreciable improvement to an existing process, material, device, product or service through scientific or technological changes; or

(d) use science or technology to duplicate the effect of an existing process, material, device, product or service in a new or appreciably improved way."

The above list is not exhaustive and only serves to indicate how the advance might occur. One point it does highlight is that an advance can be made in a number of different ways.

At first glance, it would seem that a project which fails would not achieve an advance in the field and so would not be R&D for tax purposes. However, the Guidelines clarify that it is only necessary for the project to be *aimed at* achieving the advance; they explicitly state that even if a project fails the work can still be treated as an advance and as R&D for tax purposes. This means that the early stage of projects which were abandoned can be R&D for tax purposes.

Appreciable improvement

One way to make a scientific or technological advance (STA) is to make an appreciable improvement to an existing product or process or to develop a way to duplicate something which already exists in an appreciably improved way.

"Appreciable improvement" is defined (at para. 23 of the Guidelines) as an improvement which is "more than a minor or routine upgrading" and "genuine and non-trivial" in the view of a competent professional in the field.

If we take the example of making a new product, it will be necessary (in order for it to be treated as R&D) to show that the new product is more than a trivial improvement on what was possible before. This is a far lower benchmark than the idea of "advance in the field" would at first suggest.

The Guidelines state that the scale of advance which constitutes an appreciable improvement will depend on the field of science or technology to which it relates. This highlights the need to record evidence of the particular sector specialism of the individuals involved to show that they are qualified to decide whether the advance is appreciable in relation to the particular field.

It is also worth noting that an appreciable improvement can be made by adapting technology from one field into a different field.

Advance in the overall knowledge or capability of a field

An advance must be a step forward for the entire field of technology and not simply the state of knowledge or capability of the company itself. However, the overall knowledge and capability of a field includes only information that is in the public domain or readily deducible from such information. An advance which has already been achieved by others can still be the subject matter of R&D if it is not possible to work out how to achieve the result from the information in the public domain. R&D can therefore include technological "catch up" with others in the marketplace.

Similarly, if more than one company is engaged on similar work which is at the cutting edge of the field a claim could be made by more than one company.

Is it science or technology?

The advance must be an advance in science or technology. "Science" is defined (at para. 15 of the Guidelines) as "the systematic study of nature and behaviour of the physical and material universe".

The following areas are specifically excluded from the definition of science:

- the arts;
- the humanities; and
- the social sciences (including economics).

Pure mathematical advances are also excluded (para. 15) except where they are advances in "representing the nature and behaviour of the physical and material universe". An example of this would be an advance which relates to the modelling of fluid dynamics. Where claims are made for work on pure mathematical advances, the claimant must be able to show a clear link to the physical subject of the advance.

It is important that the work is systematic, and this is reflected in the record keeping requirements (see **8.5**).

"Technology" is defined (at para. 17) as "the practical application of scientific principles and knowledge", using the above definition of science. This has wide scope and can cover more than the traditional view of R&D as being undertaken in laboratories by people in white coats. It can cover any sector that uses technology in its business, such as any business manufacturing a product using technology. The development of bespoke software systems involves technology which opens up a wide range of service sectors to the relief, such as banking, insurance and actuarial services.

Practical points

It is useful to consider the baseline technology when deciding whether the project is an advance. A company can then begin to isolate the ways in which its developments are an improvement on what exists in the field.

Getting input from different members in the team is useful. This could include members from different departments, who will view the developments from different angles, and should include the sales team who will have an insight into the unique selling points of the product or process.

It is important to take a step back from the project to view it objectively. When looking back on the project it is key to consider the position the company was in at the time. This is also vital when considering the technological uncertainties (see below).

2.4.3 Scientific or technological uncertainty

In this case, the project must also involve the resolution of some scientific or technological uncertainty ("STU"). STU exists (per para. 13 of the Guidelines) when the:

> "knowledge of whether something is scientifically possible or technologically feasible, or how to achieve it in practice, is not readily available or deducible by a competent professional working in the field".

Practical points

When considering the uncertainties it is useful for the company to put itself in the position it was in at the start of the project. The scientific or technical issues which it faced in achieving its goal will give a good starting point for what the technological uncertainties were.

In looking back, the company should keep in mind the scientific or technical problems which it had to overcome during the course of the project.

System uncertainty

Scientific or technological uncertainty includes system uncertainty which arises from the complexity of a system. This can occur where there is no STU about the use of any of the individual components of a system but there is uncertainty about how the components will interact in a system. This type of STU is particularly important in software development and the development of electronic and mechanical devices.

2.4.4 Competent professional

If it is to be treated as R&D for tax purposes, the scientific or technological uncertainty must not be readily deducible in the view of a "competent professional in the field". This term is not defined further in the guidance and so takes on its general meaning. HMRC give guidance on the meaning at CIRD 81300.

The individual should have a sufficient level of skill and knowledge of the field to be able to work in it successfully. The benchmark is not the view of an expert or leader in the field but that of a competent professional.

It would be fair to expect the following characteristics to be exhibited by the competent professional:

- specific sector experience which gives him the knowledge of the baseline technology in the field;
- a track record of achievement in the field to show that he is "competent"; and

- up-to-date knowledge on the scientific and technological aspects of the field. This could take the form of continuing professional development.

In addition, evidence of specific qualifications in the area of science or technology, along with evidence of other types of training, would be advantageous to show that the individual is a "competent" professional.

Practical point

When documenting the claim to HMRC it is useful to set out the work experience, certifications, qualifications and key project experience of the competent professional involved in preparing the claim.

2.4.5 Project

To qualify as R&D the work must be systematic and planned as part of a "project". A project is defined in the BEIS guidelines (at para. 19) as follows:

> "A project consists of a number of activities conducted to a method or plan in order to achieve an advance in science or technology."

A project is made up of the activities which are carried out according to these methods or plans which serve to resolve the uncertainties in making the advance. It is this work which should qualify for the relief, along with qualifying indirect activities (see **5.7.3**). The project documentation is important in showing that the work is systematic and was carried on using a particular method. This is covered at **8.5**.

Other aspects of the definition of R&D are included in **Chapter 5** ("Calculating the benefit"), which covers the framework for determining how much of the company's activities are to be treated as R&D.

2.4.6 Illustrations of the types of project which could qualify for R&D

Sector/business	Project
Banking	Development of an internal usage software system designed to manage client funds.
Manufacturing	Improvement of a manufacturing process in terms of speeding the processing times or reducing wastage.
Architecture	Creation of appreciably improved designs for eco-homes.
Construction	Development of new and improved construction materials or methods.
Software development	Creation of a new version of a software product.
Restaurant	Development of improved cooking processes.
Food manufacture	Development of an appreciably improved system for adding water to meat products.
Brewing / distilling	Improving a distilling or brewing process.

3. Can a claim be made?

3.1 Overview of conditions

Once a company has established that it is undertaking R&D, the next step in the process is to assess whether it can make a claim for the R&D work. To do so it must meet the following conditions:

- it must be a company subject to corporation tax in the UK;
- it must be undertaking R&D which is relevant to the company;
- the expenditure for which it wants to claim must:
    - be qualifying expenditure; and
    - be allowable as a deduction for corporation tax.

There are specific anti-avoidance rules relating to R&D tax reliefs. These restrict the benefit of the relief where it is inflated by transactions which are entered into wholly or mainly to increase the benefit of the claim (CTA 2009, s. 104X and 1084).

To avoid double claiming, there are restrictions on claims being made for R&D tax reliefs and other enhanced tax reliefs (CTA 2009, s. 1040ZA and 104BA). These rules should be reviewed in detail where expenditure could qualify under more than one scheme.

This chapter looks in more detail at the general conditions for a claim.

3.2 Company subject to CT

The R&D expenditure reliefs are only available to companies. A company is defined as:

- any body corporate, including entities limited by share capital and by guarantee; and
- any unincorporated association.

The definition does not include:

- a partnership or LLP;

- a local authority; or
- a local authority association.

Companies can carry out R&D as a member of a partnership (which means that the R&D activity may be undertaken through an LLP, for example) but in these circumstances only a corporate member will benefit from the R&D relief.

The company must be subject to UK corporation tax but this can include:

- a foreign branch of a UK company if it is within the charge to UK tax;
- a UK branch of a foreign company if it is within the charge to UK tax; and
- a company which is a member of a partnership which undertakes qualifying R&D activities.

Law: CTA 2010, s. 1121

3.3 Relevant R&D

Relevant R&D for a company is defined as R&D:

"(a) related to the trade carried on by the company; or

(b) from which it is intended that a trade to be carried on by the company will be derived."

There is further guidance in the legislation on what could constitute R&D related to the trade, including:

- R&D which may lead to or facilitate an extension of the trade; and
- medical research related to the workers of the company.

It should be noted that these are examples for guidance only and are not exhaustive.

This condition means that companies which do not carry on a trade – such as property rental companies and companies which purely hold investments – cannot make a claim. The definition of a trade is not considered here but further guidance on this can be found in the *Business Income Manual* (beginning at BIM 20000).

Law: CTA 2009, s. 1042

3.4 Expenditure criteria

3.4.1 Overview

There are various criteria relating to the type of expenditure which can qualify for the relief. Specifically:

- the expenditure must be qualifying expenditure; and
- it must be allowable as a deduction in calculating trading profits.

3.4.2 Qualifying expenditure

The legislation sets out specifically what expenditure qualifies for the relief. In summary this includes:

- staffing costs (see **5.4.3**);
- software (see **5.4.4**);
- consumable items or transformable stores, for example water, heat and power (see **5.4.4**);
- externally provided workers – broadly these are staff provided by other parties, such as employment agencies or other group companies (see **5.4.5**);
- payments made as part of clinical trials (see **5.4.6**);
- subcontracted R&D – but the rules are complex here and differ depending on whether the company is an SME or not (see **Chapter 4**); and
- contributions to independent research (see **5.6.3**).

The rules for the calculation of qualifying expenditure are complex, and the type of expenditure that can be claimed differs between the schemes; this is covered in more detail in **Chapter 5**.

Law: CTA 2009, s. 104C-104L, 1051-1053

3.4.3 Allowable as a deduction in calculating the profits of the trade

The expenditure must also be allowable as a deduction in computing the profits of the trade for corporation tax purposes.

Importantly for many R&D companies this can include expenditure which is incurred before the trade has begun ("pre-trading expenditure"). For most companies the expenditure is treated as occurring on the first day of the trade; however, there are special rules for SME companies (see **Chapter 4** for a definition).

SME companies can accelerate the tax relief for their R&D expenditure and can even cash in any losses for the R&D tax credit (see **Chapter 5**).

Not capital

To qualify for the relief, the expenditure must not be capital in nature. The difference between capital and revenue expenditure can be complex and is not covered in detail here. There is extensive guidance on this in the *Business Income Manual* (beginning at BIM 35000).

There are specific rules which relate to expenditure that is capitalised as an "intangible" in the company accounts. Under these rules, R&D tax reliefs can be claimed – and a deduction for the capitalised "intangible" expenditure can be taken – where the expenditure:

- is on R&D;
- is not of a capital nature; and
- has been taken into account by the company in determining the value of an intangible asset.

This cannot be applied where either a tax deduction has been made for the expenditure for an earlier accounting period or R&D tax reliefs have been claimed in respect of the expenditure in a previous period.

Where a deduction is taken under these rules, there is no tax deduction for the writing down of the asset in the future. This means that the amortisation of the asset over time must be disallowed in the tax computation of the company.

Law: FA 2004, s. 53; CTA 2009, s. 1308

3.5 Conclusion

This chapter has considered whether a claim can be made for R&D tax credits. The next chapter will explain the scheme under which a claim can be made. The additional requirements of the SME scheme will be considered, as this is the most beneficial route.

4. Under which scheme should a claim be made?

4.1 Introduction

Once a company has determined that it can make an R&D claim, the next step is to decide under which scheme the claim should be made. The SME scheme is far more generous than the research and development expenditure credit (RDEC) scheme and the RDEC scheme for SMEs (covering types of SME expenditure not covered by the SME scheme).

Extra support is given to SMEs as they are perceived to be essential to driving innovation, economic growth and job creation, and as they generally find sources of funding harder to come by. It is therefore important to understand whether or not the claim is made under the SME scheme.

The first consideration is the size of the enterprise. An enterprise is an SME where it has *fewer than* 500 employees and where one of the following criteria is met:

- annual turnover not exceeding 100 million euros; or
- balance sheet total not exceeding 86 million euros.

This calculation can be complex, especially in situations involving venture capital investment or where individuals own more than one enterprise, and is considered in more detail below. However, the size of the enterprise is not the only factor that will determine the scheme under which a claim can be made. For expenditure to qualify for the SME scheme the following further conditions must also be met:

- the company must be a going concern;
- the project must not exceed a cap of €7.5 million of R&D aid;
- the R&D must not have been subcontracted to the company;
- another party must not be subsidising the R&D expenditure;

- the company must not have received a "notified state aid" in respect of the project.

If the expenditure fails to meet all of these conditions then the expenditure may still qualify under the RDEC scheme. In fact, it is possible to make a claim under both the SME scheme and the RDEC scheme for SMEs for the same project.

A key exception to the above rules relates to insurance companies. Any company which carries on a life assurance business is automatically treated as a large company irrespective of its size.

Law: CTA 2009, s. 104U, 1081

4.2 What is an SME?

The definition of an SME is set out primarily through an EC "Recommendation" (2003/361/EC) with amendments made as part the tax legislation; importantly the limits are double those in the original Recommendation. The Recommendation is reproduced as **Appendix 2**.

As set out above, an enterprise is an SME where it has *fewer than* 500 employees and where one of the following criteria is met:

- annual turnover not exceeding 100 million euros; or
- balance sheet total not exceeding 86 million euros.

This is a simple test to apply to single companies which are independent of other enterprises (called "autonomous enterprises"). However, the considerations become more complex where:

- another enterprise can control the company (linked enterprise);
- the company can control another enterprise (linked enterprise);
- another enterprise owns at least 25% of the capital or shares of the company (partner enterprise);
- the company owns at least 25% of the capital or shares of another enterprise (partner enterprise);

- a person (or a group of persons acting together) controls the company and another enterprise in the same or adjacent market (linked enterprise) (see **4.5.3** below); or
- public bodies have invested in the enterprise.

Law: CTA 2009, s. 1119-1122
Guidance: EC Recommendation (2003/361/EC)

4.3 Definition of enterprise

Although the R&D relief only applies to companies, it is important to note that the term "enterprise" is more widely defined for the purposes of the Recommendation, as follows:

> "An enterprise is considered to be any entity engaged in an economic activity, irrespective of its legal form. This includes, in particular, self-employed persons and family businesses engaged in craft or other activities, and partnerships or associations regularly engaged in an economic activity."

A careful consideration of the ownership structure must be made, taking into account not just companies but any type of enterprise undertaking economic activity. HMRC pick out this wide-ranging definition in their guidance, stating that "for example, a company owned by a large charity can fail the SME test, because the charity is an enterprise."

This definition can add significant complexity in deciding whether a company can be treated as an SME and can give rise to some unexpected results.

Guidance: EC Recommendation (2003/361/EC), art. 1; CIRD 91200

4.4 Cases of uncertainty

Where it is not possible to determine the status of a company it is still possible, under the Recommendation, for the company to make a declaration that it is an SME. This declaration can be made in good faith where there is reason to believe that the company is an SME. The guidance states:

> "Enterprises may make a declaration of status as an autonomous enterprise, partner enterprise or linked enterprise, including the data regarding the ceilings set out in

> Article 2. The declaration may be made even if the capital is spread in such a way that it is not possible to determine exactly by whom it is held, in which case the enterprise may declare in good faith that it can legitimately presume that it is not owned as to 25 % or more by one enterprise or jointly by enterprises linked to one another. Such declarations are made without prejudice to the checks and investigations provided for by national or Community rules."

This is reflected in the HMRC guidance:

> "In some cases the spread of capital may mean that it is not possible for an enterprise to determine with certainty that it is not owned 25% or more by another enterprise or jointly by linked enterprises. Where there is reason to believe that a company is an SME the company may make a declaration in good faith about its status regarding autonomy, partner and linked enterprises."

Guidance: EC Recommendation (2003/361/EC), art. 3; CIRD 91700

4.5 Linked enterprises

4.5.1 Overview

A company is linked with another enterprise where one enterprise has what could be broadly defined as control of the other. The EC Recommendation states that entities are linked where:

(a) an enterprise has a majority of the shareholders' or members' voting rights in another enterprise;

(b) an enterprise has the right to appoint or remove a majority of the members of the administrative, management or supervisory body of another enterprise;

(c) an enterprise has the right to exercise a dominant influence over another enterprise pursuant to a contract entered into with that enterprise or to a provision in its memorandum or articles of association;

(d) an enterprise, which is a shareholder in or member of another enterprise, controls alone, pursuant to an agreement with other shareholders in or members of that enterprise, a majority of shareholders' or members' voting rights in that enterprise.

In the case of certain specified investors, the Recommendation states that there should be no presumption of dominant influence where the enterprise is not involved directly or indirectly in the management of the enterprise. See **4.8** below for details of specified investors.

When deciding whether an entity is linked you should first consider the definition given by the EC Recommendation and the particular facts of the case. HMRC's published view on the interpretation of the EC Recommendation is given in **4.5.2** below.

4.5.2 HMRC's Interpretation

HMRC's guidance states that the conditions of being a linked enterprise are "...tests of 'control'; enterprises are linked if one of them directly or indirectly controls, or has the capacity to control, the affairs of the other". Control is not specifically defined in the Recommendation. It is defined elsewhere in the tax legislation but these definitions have a different application and should not be used for interpreting control for the purposes of deciding if an enterprise is an SME.

HMRC consider that control should be defined widely to include "any arrangements whereby a party can secure that a company will operate in accordance with its wishes".

HMRC guidance goes on to state that:

> "... we can say that we regard all of the following as constituting control, without intending this in any way as an exhaustive list:
>
> - Possession of a majority of the voting share capital.
> - Being entitled to acquire the majority of the voting share capital.
> - Being able to appoint or dismiss the majority of any supervisory or executive officers.
> - Being able to control key aspects of the business, or prevent any material exercise of discretion in such areas by the executives."

Particular care should be taken when deciding whether the investment of venture capitalists ("VCs") cause a company to exceed the SME limits, since account has to be taken also of the venture capitalist's other controlled investments in making the aggregation.

Guidance: CIRD 91600, 92500

4.5.3 Enterprises linked by individuals (or a group of individuals)

It is possible for enterprises to be linked by an individual or group of individuals; for example, where two companies are owned by one person but are not within a group of companies.

Where this is the case, the enterprises are only treated as being linked if they are in the same or adjacent markets. They will, however, be linked even if the activity in the same or adjacent market only makes up part of the enterprise's activities. Broadly speaking, two markets are treated as being adjacent to one another where they are directly up or downstream from each other. This can occur where one market supplies products or services to the other.

Example 1

Company A produces parts used in the manufacture of cars.

Company B manufactures cars.

These companies are in adjacent markets.

Example 2

Company C develops gaming products for children.

Company D provides professional services to individuals.

These companies should not be in adjacent markets.

4.6 Partnership enterprises

4.6.1 Overview

This test is more narrowly defined than linked enterprises. It applies to situations where the entities are not linked and looks specifically at capital ownership and voting rights. To be a partner enterprise one enterprise (the upstream enterprise) must hold at least 25% of the capital or voting rights of another enterprise (the downstream enterprise).

Where an enterprise has other linked enterprises it must aggregate the interests in all linked enterprises in deciding if the entity is a partner enterprise.

4.6.2 Capital

"Capital" is not defined specifically and so is open to interpretation.

HMRC take the view that it can be construed more widely than simply the ordinary share capital of the company, and "can include preference shares, or loan finance of a capital nature, particularly if that loan finance is convertible to equity at some point".

Guidance: CIRD 92300

4.6.3 Ownership by a public body

A company cannot be an SME if 25% or more of the capital or voting rights are directly or indirectly controlled, jointly or individually, by one or more public bodies. This means that if any number of public bodies hold 25% or more of the capital or voting rights in total, even if they individually hold only a very small proportion, then the company cannot be an SME.

The interest of a public body is excluded if it falls within one of the categories of specified investors listed at **4.8**.

4.6.4 Exemption

An enterprise will not be treated as a partner enterprise if the investment is made by certain types of specified investors (again, see **4.8**).

4.7 Calculation of limits

4.7.1 General principle

For autonomous enterprises, those which have no linked or partner enterprises, the limits are simply compared to the figures for the enterprise. Where a company has a linked or partner enterprise, the totals of the company and the linked or partner enterprise must be aggregated, the former in their entirety and the latter proportionately (see below for more details).

4.7.2 Aggregation

The proportion of the figures of other enterprises which must be aggregated depends on whether they are partner or linked enterprises:

- 100% of the figures of linked enterprises are aggregated;
- a proportion of the figures of partner enterprises are aggregated equal to the proportion of the interest in the other enterprise.

Where the percentage of capital or voting rights is different, the higher figure should be used for the purposes of the aggregation. Where a partnership enterprise has its own linked or partner enterprises these should be aggregated before applying the appropriate proportion.

Example

A Ltd owns 100% of the share capital of B Ltd and 30% of the share capital and voting rights of C Ltd. B Ltd is treated as a linked enterprise and C Ltd is treated as a partner enterprise (as the other shareholder has the majority of the rights over the company).

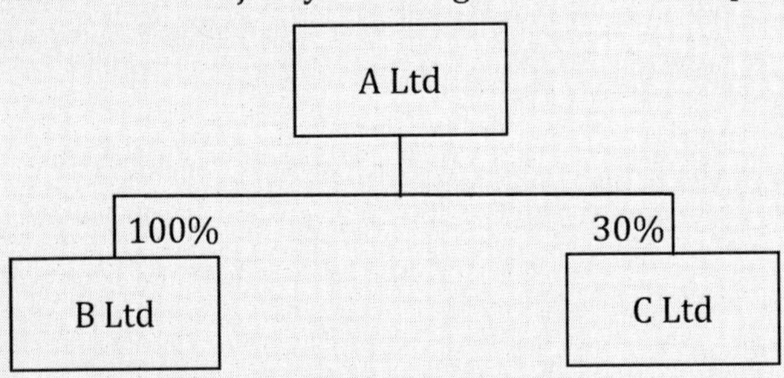

The figures for each company are as follows:

	Staff	Turnover (€)	Balance Sheet (€)
A Ltd	100	1,500,000	500,000
B Ltd	150	500,000	250,000
C Ltd	100	1,000,000	100,000

For the purposes of deciding whether A Ltd is an SME, 100% of the totals of A Ltd and B Ltd and 30% of the totals of C Ltd are aggregated.

	Staff	Turnover (€)	Balance Sheet (€)
A Ltd	100	1,500,000	500,000
B Ltd	150	500,000	250,000
C Ltd	30	300,000	30,000
Total	280	2,300,000	700,000

4.7.3 *Which figures are used?*

The EC Recommendation suggests that, wherever possible, a company's accounts should be used. However, HMRC reserve the right to investigate in more detail where the figures included in the accounts give an "unjust" result. For group companies, consolidated accounts should be used to ascertain the relevant levels.

Where a company does not have accounts because the accounts have not been finalised, an estimate of the figures can be used. This relaxation will not apply to the company making the claim as accounts are required in order to submit the corporation tax return including the claim. It could, however, apply to newly formed linked or partner enterprises.

For the financial tests it will be necessary to calculate the Euro equivalent figures where the figures are given in other currencies, as is likely to be the case.

Guidance: CIRD 91800

4.7.4 *Staff calculation*

The staff number includes individuals working in or on behalf of the enterprise in the period and is based on the number of full time "person years" (or "annual worker units"). It is neither the total number of staff employed in the year nor the highest in the year. Where individuals work part time or do not work for the entire year, they are counted as the appropriate proportion of "person years".

For these purposes, the following should be included:

- employees;
- individuals seconded to the business;
- owner-managers; and
- partners (except sleeping partners not involved in regular activity in the business).

The following should be excluded:

- apprentices;
- students engaged on a vocational training contract; and
- periods of maternity or paternity leave (but see below).

Where an individual is on maternity or paternity leave for part of the year, only the period on leave is excluded from the calculation.

Example

A Ltd has 500 employees on its balance sheet date as at 31 December. Of these, 20 employees were only employed from 1 July, 50 employees work part time for the whole year (17.5 hours a week), and 430 employees were employed full time for the whole year.

A Ltd has 465 employees based on annual worker units.

4.7.5 Turnover

The turnover limit is based on a year so the figure must be increased or reduced accordingly if the period of account is longer or shorter than a year.

The limit excludes VAT and other indirect taxes.

4.7.6 Calculating the balance sheet total

The balance sheet total of a company is the gross amount of assets on its balance sheet in its financial statements.

4.8 Specified investors

4.8.1 Overview

A number of enterprises have special rules within the Recommendation which affects how and if they are aggregated.

Such enterprises are here referred to as "specified investors" (or "SI"s). They are seen as drivers of economic growth so they are not included in the aggregation in specific cases, provided that they are not linked to the enterprise, either individually or jointly (see **4.5**). These investors are as follows:

- public investment corporations;
- venture capital ("VC") companies;
- individuals or groups of individuals acting as "business angels" if the total investment is less than 1.25 million euros;
- universities or non-profit research centres;
- institutional investors, such as regional growth funds; and
- certain local authorities.

This relaxation could be important where a VC makes an investment into a company including the requirement that the company signs an investment agreement to protect the interests of the VC. The terms of the investment agreement could be deemed to give rise to dominant influence to the VC, depending on the facts (see **4.5.1**). Where the figures of the VC are aggregated with the company the SME limit may be exceeded. It may be possible, depending on the facts, to argue that the VC is not involved in the management of the business and so retain SME status.

When reviewing HMRC's guidance on whether an entity could be treated as a VC, consideration should be given to the decision in *Pyreos Ltd*. In this case, the taxpayer successfully argued that an entity should be treated as a venture capital company. In addition, where considering whether an entity is a venture capital company or an institutional investor, consideration should be given to *Monitor Audio Ltd*. In the *Monitor Audio* case, the Tribunal allowed an SME claim on the basis that a subsidiary of the RBS Group could be treated as an institutional investor. HMRC's guidance on the meaning of institutional investor can be found at CIRD 92200.

Cases: *Pyreos Ltd v HMRC* [2015] UKFTT 123 (TC); *Monitor Audio Ltd v HMRC* [2015] UKFTT 357 (TC)

4.8.2 Venture capital companies

Many companies, especially those in the early development stages, look for investment from VC companies. There is a specific exemption for the interests of VC companies from aggregation as partner enterprises. In looking at this, it is important to review all agreements which the company enters into with its VC investors in order to ensure that the VC cannot be treated as controlling the enterprise, which would in turn necessitate treatment as a linked enterprise (see **4.5**).

A VC company is not defined further in the Recommendation but HMRC give guidance on their interpretation of what constitutes a VC company. The VC company does not in fact need to be a company but could (for example) be a limited partnership vehicle. The HMRC guidance defines a VC as follows.

> "[A VC] is an institution providing, as its specialised business, finance to start-up or developing businesses, where a fairly high degree of risk is involved. The investment would be likely to be in the form of equity, but may it be supported by loans. One would expect a high return commensurate with the level of risk, and the company to be looking to realise its capital in successful investments as part of the overall business.
>
> We would also expect the company to make a significant number of investments in different companies so as to provide the spread of risk that one would associate with the carrying on of a business, rather than simply the making of one or more speculative investments."

The HMRC guidance suggests that the investment should not be simply an isolated investment made by the enterprise but that there should generally be a track record of similar investments. Where the investment is made as the start of a series of transactions, the company should be able to provide evidence of the means and of the intention to follow the investment plan through. As mentioned at **4.8.1** above, where VC companies are involved, consideration should be given to the *Pyreos* and *Monitor Audio* cases.

Guidance: CIRD 92100

4.9 Changes of status

4.9.1 Transitional rules

There are transitional rules which are designed to smooth the transition between the SME and RDEC schemes. Where a company exceeds the SME limits at its balance sheet date it is not treated as being large until it is repeated the following period. This also works in reverse, so a company which was large but falls below the SME limits at its balance sheet date will not be treated as an SME until this is repeated for a second year.

Example 1

A Ltd is a singleton company which is growing and takes on more staff to deal with the increasing demand for its product. A Ltd has the following annual worker unit totals:

31 December 2016 – 450

31 December 2017 – 510

31 December 2018 – 600

The turnover and balance sheet totals both fall below the thresholds for SME status.

A Ltd is an SME for the periods ended 31 December 2016 and 31 December 2017. It will be large for the year to 31 December 2018.

Example 2

B Ltd has lost a key customer and is forced to let staff go as part of an internal restructuring of its manufacturing and administrative functions. B Ltd has the following staff totals:

31 December 2016 – 600

31 December 2017 – 490

31 December 2018 – 450

The turnover and balance sheet total both fall below the thresholds for SME status.

B Ltd is large for the periods ended 31 December 2016 and 31 December 2017. It will be an SME for the year to 31 December 2018.

4.9.2 *Exclusion from the transitional rules*

The transitional rules do not apply where an enterprise ("C Ltd" in the example below):

- is an SME if linked and partner enterprises are disregarded;
- exceeds the thresholds as a result of aggregating with linked or partner enterprises which exceed the SME limits if C Ltd is disregarded.

An example of this could be where a company has been taken over by a large group.

Note that this exclusion to the transitional rules does not apply to companies which are becoming SME as a result of no longer aggregating linked or partner enterprises. An example of this would be a situation where a company is sold by a large group to individual investors. In these circumstances the normal transitional rules apply.

Example 1

C Ltd has been making strong progress but in order to reach new markets it sells 60% of its share capital to a larger competitor (D Ltd). The sale of the shares occurs on 1 January 2017.

Total employee numbers included in the aggregation are as follows at balance sheet date:

31 December 2016 – 100

31 December 2017 – 700 (100 employees of C Ltd and 600 employees of D Ltd)

31 December 2018 – 705 (100 employees of C Ltd and 605 employees of D Ltd)

The turnover and balance sheet totals of C Ltd both fall below the thresholds for SME status but the combined totals for the two companies exceed the threshold in the periods ended 31 December 2017 and 2018.

C Ltd is an SME for the year ended 31 December 2016 but large for the year ended 31 December 2017 (as there is no period of grace) and for the year ended 31 December 2018.

Example 2

E Ltd has been part of a large group for some time. The owners of E Ltd agree with the management to undertake a management buy-out. The sale of the shares occurs on 1 January 2017. E Ltd has the following employee totals at balance sheet date:

31 December 2016 – 700 (100 employees of E Ltd and 600 employees in the rest of the group)

31 December 2017 – 100

31 December 2018 – 100

The turnover and balance sheet total for E Ltd both fall below the thresholds for SME status.

E Ltd is large for the years ended 31 December 2016 and 31 December 2017 (even though it meets the SME limits at the balance sheet date) but is an SME for the year ended 31 December 2018.

Law: CTA 2009, s. 1120

4.10 Further conditions of the SME scheme

4.10.1 Going concern

A company may only make a claim under the various SME scheme reliefs where it is a "going concern". For this purpose a company is a going concern if it:

- prepared its last published accounts on a going concern basis and nothing in the accounts indicates that the company is only a going concern because of repayment of the R&D relief; and
- has not entered into liquidation or administration.

The company must be a going concern at the time of the claim and at the time of payment of the credit. So if a company has made a claim at a time when it is a going concern, but it ceases to be a going concern before the payment, HMRC will not repay the R&D tax relief. However, if the tax credit is paid and the company subsequently ceases to be a going concern, the credit should not be clawed back.

Law: CTA 2009, s. 1046

4.10.2 Cap on total aid

A company cannot claim relief under the SME scheme if it has already received more than 7.5 million euros of R&D relief for a particular project. R&D relief for this purpose only includes relief for SMEs (under CTA 2009, Pt. 13, Ch. 2) and vaccine relief for large companies (under CTA 2009, Pt. 13, Ch. 7) up to its abolition. The method of calculation of the aid was amended by FA 2016.

Where expenditure cannot qualify for the SME scheme because it has exceeded the cap, it may qualify for the RDEC scheme for SMEs (see **Chapter 7**).

The BEIS guidelines (at para. 19) give the following guidance on the meaning of a project.

> "A project consists of a number of activities conducted to a method or plan in order to achieve an advance in science or technology. It is important to get the boundaries of the project correct. It should encompass all the activities which collectively serve to resolve the scientific or technological uncertainty associated with achieving the advance, so it could include a number of different sub-projects."

It is important to distinguish here between the technological goals and the commercial goals of the project. A wider commercial project may include more than one technological project which each achieves a separate advance in science or technology. The Guidelines also state:

> "A project may itself be part of a larger commercial project, but that does not make the parts of the commercial project that do not address scientific or technological uncertainty into R&D."

Law: CTA 2009, s. 1113-1118

4.10.3 Not subsidised

A company can only claim for expenditure under the SME scheme which it has funded itself (this is not the case under the RDEC scheme). Subsidised expenditure can qualify for relief under the RDEC scheme.

Expenditure is subsidised if:

- a grant or subsidy is received in respect of the expenditure;
- the expenditure is met directly or indirectly by another person; or
- any notified state aid is received for a project (see below).

In some cases this can be a complex issue. A distinction should be made between work that has been subsidised by another party and where another party has simply paid for the product. It is important to consider the contractual terms in detail before embarking on such a project to ensure that they properly reflect the nature of the transaction and do not unnecessarily prevent a company from appropriately claiming relief later.

Practical points

This is an important and complex area which should be carefully considered. It is important to examine the relationship between the parties in detail, in terms of both the practical and contractual arrangements. It may be appropriate to seek additional professional advice on this point.

Law: CTA2009, s. 1052(6), 1053(5), 1138

4.10.4 No notified state aid

The R&D relief for SMEs is very beneficial and as a result it is treated as a "notified state aid" ("NSA"). An NSA is aid given by a government which must be notified to, and approved by, the European Commission. If another state aid (other than the SME R&D relief) has been claimed for a "project", a claim cannot be made under the SME scheme for *any expenditure on the project.* The company should consider a claim for relief under the less beneficial RDEC scheme for SMEs for the project.

To reiterate, if an NSA is received on any aspect of a project then none of the expenditure on the project can qualify for the SME scheme. This is different from the rules for subsidised expenditure, which only exclude the subsidised costs from the relief. It is important to consider the extent of the "project" as defined by the BEIS guidelines (see **2.4.5** above) to see whether more than one project is being undertaken.

Not all aid given by the government is "notified" and HMRC give limited guidance on NSAs at CIRD 81670. Once an NSA is given it is not possible to repay it in order to make a claim under the SME scheme. Accordingly careful consideration should be given to deciding which aid to apply for and a detailed analysis of the costs and benefits of each should be undertaken.

Law: CTA 2009, s. 1138(1)(a)
Guidance: CIRD 81670

4.10.5 Not contracted out to the company

A company cannot claim under the SME scheme if the work it is undertaking is subcontracted to it by another party. If the work is subcontracted to the SME then it may be possible to claim under the RDEC scheme for SMEs (see **Chapter 7**).

Practical points

Once more, this is an important and complex area which should be carefully considered. It is important to examine the relationship between the parties in detail, both in terms of the practical and contractual arrangements. The definition of subcontracting is relevant both to whether a company can claim under the SME scheme and to whether payments made to contractors can be treated as qualifying expenditure. It may be appropriate to seek additional professional advice on this point.

The term "subcontracted" is not specifically defined in the legislation and so should take its normal meaning. HMRC guidance on the meaning of subcontracting states:

> "Where one company engages another company to carry out R&D activity on the first company's behalf in exchange for payment, with the first company having rights to the

intellectual property resulting from the R&D then that is subcontracting of the R&D to the second company."

This is distinguished from the provision of services or personal employment, where a company or person is simply providing services rather than undertaking a specific part of the project.

The guidance picks out the following further examples of arrangements between parties involved in R&D projects.

> "There are obviously a considerable variety of possible contractual arrangements. Some examples are:
>
> - Where a company carries out R&D on its own account (retaining use of the intellectual property in the work) and simply receives a subsidy from another entity, this is not subcontracting – it is subsidised expenditure.
> - Where two companies are both carrying out R&D on the same subject they may decide to pursue the R&D jointly with each making a contribution and each free to enjoy any fruits of the R&D. This is collaborative research and each company would potentially be eligible for R&D relief on its share of the qualifying expenditure.
> - Where one company carrying out R&D pays another company for the provision of workers, or materials this is not subcontracting of the R&D."

Subcontracting should therefore be distinguished from the following arrangements between parties involved in R&D:

- **Subsidised R&D** – where one party carries out R&D on its own behalf but is subsidised by another party, in which case the costs could qualify under the RDEC scheme for SMEs (see **7.3**);
- **Collaborative R&D** – where two (or more) parties undertake R&D on the same subject jointly, with each making a contribution and each able to exploit the IP. In this case, each company could claim under the SME scheme.

In deciding whether the work is subcontracted, the guidance states that:

> "Each case will need to be judged on its particular facts. As part of any examination it may be useful to examine the degree of autonomy enjoyed by the person engaged, the ownership of intellectual property, and the economic risk in any arrangements."

In summary, this is a highly contested area but the following are indicators that a company is acting as a subcontractor in cases where it is working on behalf of another enterprise:

- it will not retain the intellectual property arising from the work;
- it is undertaking work that represents a discrete element of the project;
- it is relatively autonomous in its actions;
- it will not benefit economically from the success of the wider project; and
- it bears economic risk in relation to its element of the work but not the wider project.

Not all factors may be relevant to every case, so a detailed analysis of each should be made and consideration given to all of the facts.

Law: CTA 2009, s. 1052(5), 1053(4)
Guidance: CIRD 84250

5. Calculating the benefit

5.1 Introduction

Once a company has determined that the work it is undertaking may qualify for R&D tax reliefs it will want to know how much tax it can save. As mentioned earlier, this depends on the scheme under which a claim is being made. The SME scheme is far more beneficial than the other schemes, so a careful review of the criteria should be made to check whether the tests of this relief are met.

5.2 SME scheme

5.2.1 Overview

The two ways in which a company gets relief for its R&D expenditure are as:

- an additional tax deduction; or
- a tax credit.

The additional tax deduction increases the tax deduction available for the expenditure, giving rise to a "super-deduction". The current rate is 230% which means that a company gets a tax deduction at more than double the rate of tax relief for qualifying expenditure. For example, if a company spends £100,000 on qualifying expenditure, the super-deduction will be £230,000. This is made up of a deduction of £100,000 already included in the profit and loss account and £130,000 of additional tax relief (an enhancement of 130%).

If the company makes a loss (after taking into account the super-deduction) then it can claim a tax credit. Essentially, a company can claim tax relief, even where it is not paying corporation tax, in return for surrendering its tax losses. The "cash back" claim is at 14.5% of the losses. This may be compared to the cash value of the super-deduction, if relieved against profits, of 19% (assuming the claimant company pays tax at 19%). A decision must therefore be made whether to "cash in" the losses for the tax credit at a lower rate or to carry forward the losses to use against future profits. In other words, a company may get more benefit where the losses can be carried forward, but this needs to be weighed against the benefit of the additional cash which can be used within the business at an earlier stage.

Example

A Ltd invests heavily in the development of a new product. It employs four new developers and after an analysis of the work undertaken, it is decided that £200,000 of the costs of the development is qualifying expenditure for the year ended 31 March 2019. A Ltd is not able to use the losses through carry back of the losses or through group or consortium relief.

The investment in the new product meant that the company made a loss before calculating the enhanced R&D relief of £100,000. The loss after calculating the enhancement for the R&D is £360,000. This loss could be carried forward against future profits. If these losses are set off against profits, they could be relieved at 19% (or such rate as may be applicable when the losses are utilised) and the benefit would be £68,400 (at 19%). The cash benefit would be realised when the tax payment for the profits, against which the losses are offset, falls due. If the losses were offset in full against profits from the year ended 31 March 2020 then the cash benefit is only received on 1 January 2021 (assuming the company is not paying its corporation tax by instalments).

If the losses are cashed in for an R&D tax credit then the repayment would be £52,200, which is usually receivable within a month of the claim. The benefit from "cashing in" the losses is lower but the timing of the tax relief is accelerated. The cash flow benefit is likely to be greater, of course, when profits are unlikely to arise for a long period.

Further consideration should be given to the fact that the rate of corporation tax is due to reduce from 1 April 2020 to 17% (as currently enacted).

The rate of enhancement has changed over the years. The rates applicable are set out below to assist in calculating claims for previous years. It was announced in the 2018 Budget that, from April 2020, the tax credit would be capped at three times the company's total PAYE and National Insurance contribution for a year. At the time of writing, the government were consulting on the mechanism of the proposed cap.

Financial Year Ended	SME Enhancement	Percentage of Losses	Maximum Credit as Percentage of Qualifying Spend
31 March 2019	130%	14.5%	33.35%
31 March 2018	130%	14.5%	33.35%
31 March 2017	130%	14.5%	33.35%
31 March 2016	130%	14.5%	33.35%
31 March 2015	125%	14.5%	32.625%
31 March 2014	125%	11%	24.75%
31 March 2013	125%	11%	24.75%

Law: CTA 2009, Pt. 13, Ch. 2

5.2.2 *Calculating the tax credit*

The company surrenders its losses for a repayment of 14.5% of its trade losses. The losses which the company can surrender are equal to the lower of:

- unrelieved trading losses of the period; or
- 230% of the qualifying expenditure (lower rates apply before 1 April 2015).

The losses are unrelieved if:

- they could not be set off against profits in the same period (the company did not have other types of profits in the year);
- they have not been used in another way (for example, carried back against profits of a prior period); and
- they have not been surrendered by group or consortium relief.

These losses are termed the "surrenderable losses". Once the losses are surrendered they cannot be carried forward to offset against future profits of the trade.

Example (continued from Example at 5.2.1 above)

A Ltd decides to cash in its losses for the R&D tax credit.

Loss for year before R&D relief	(£100,000)
Enhanced expenditure	(£260,000)
Loss after R&D relief	(£360,000)
Lower of:	
Surrenderable loss	£360,000
230% of qualifying expenditure	£460,000

Tax credit = £52,200 (£360,000 x 14.5%).

The entire loss of £360,000 is extinguished in claiming the R&D tax credit and cannot be carried forward for use against future profits.

5.2.3 Special rules for pre-trading expenditure

Generally, where a company incurs expenditure before it begins to trade, it obtains tax relief for the expenditure when it starts to trade. This would prevent companies which undertake R&D in preparation for beginning to trade from claiming the R&D tax credit. Special rules are therefore included in the legislation which treat the pre-trading expenditure as though it creates a loss of the trade for the period in which the expenditure is incurred.

Law: CTA 2009, s. 1045-1048, 1137

5.3 Large scheme

The large super-deduction scheme, and large super-deduction scheme for SMEs, remained broadly unchanged from when they were introduced in 2002 until 31 March 2013. During this period it was not possible to claim tax credit relief. A super-deduction was available at a lower rate than under the SME scheme.

For expenditure incurred from 1 April 2013 to 31 March 2016, companies could choose whether to claim under the super-deduction scheme or under the new "R&D expenditure credit"

("RDEC") rules. From 1 April 2016 the large super-deduction scheme was replaced with the RDEC rules. The RDEC scheme is covered in more detail in **Chapters 6 and 7**.

5.4 Qualifying expenditure – both schemes

5.4.1 Introduction

Various categories of expenditure can qualify for R&D tax relief. These differ significantly between the SME and RDEC scheme so care should be taken to ascertain the correct scheme before starting to calculate the qualifying expenditure. See **Chapter 4** for guidance as to whether to claim under the SME or RDEC scheme.

As a general rule, expenditure which is capital in nature will not qualify for the R&D expenditure reliefs. A detailed analysis of how to decide whether expenditure is capital in nature is outside the scope of this book, but as a broad guide expenditure giving rise to an asset which has an enduring benefit within the business is likely to be capital. Capital expenditure may qualify for research and development allowances (see **Chapter 9**).

There are specific rules for "intangible" assets which are discussed further at **3.4.3**.

5.4.2 Connected persons

The amount of expenditure which qualifies for R&D tax relief can depend on whether the company making the claim is "connected" to the entity to which it is making the payment. The types of expenditure are:

- externally provided workers;
- subcontracted R&D; and
- contributions to independent research.

The definition of "connected" is widely framed and can cover a range of relationships, so care should be taken in deciding whether two entities or individuals are connected. The definition of "connected persons" is summarised in the table below:

Relationship	Definition of connection

Company with another company	• one person ("A") controls both;
	• A controls one company and persons connected to A control another;
	• A controls one company and A with those connected with A control another;
	• a group of two or more persons have control of two companies and the group:
	    ○ is made up of the same persons; or
	    ○ could be regarded as the same if one or more members of either group is replaced by a person with whom the member is connected.

Company with another person	• A has control of the company; or • A together with persons connected with them control the company.
Two or more persons controlling a company	If acting together to control a company, persons are connected with each other and with any persons acting on direction of any of them to secure or exercise control of the company.
Individual to individual	An individual ("A") is connected with another individual ("B") if: • A is B's spouse or civil partner; • A is a relative of B; • A is the spouse or civil partner of a relative of B; • A is a relative of B's spouse or civil partner; or • A is the spouse or civil partner of a relative of B's spouse or civil partner.

In addition a trustee of a settlement is treated as connected with various parties involved with the settlement.

A person is treated as controlling a company where he can ensure that the affairs of the company are carried out in accordance with his wishes:

- by means of shareholding or voting rights; or
- as a result of powers in the articles of association or other document regulating the company.

"Relative" is defined for these purposes as a lineal descendent, ancestor, brother or sister.

Law: CTA 2010, s. 1122-1124

5.4.3 Staffing costs

The largest element of an R&D claim is usually the staffing costs, these being the main costs of most IP development businesses. As many employees generally do not work on R&D all of the time it is important to apportion their costs between qualifying and non-qualifying activities, as discussed more fully below.

The following elements of an employee or director's benefit package could qualify for the relief:

1. Money earnings which are paid because of the individual's employment.
2. Expense payments made to reimburse individuals for costs they have incurred (this does not include purchases made on a company credit card).
3. Employer's National Insurance contributions (or equivalent payments made in the EEA or Switzerland).
4. Employer's pension contributions.

Benefits in kind, such as company cars, do not now qualify for the relief.

In the majority of cases, especially in small companies, individuals will not be fully committed to undertaking R&D. In these cases an apportionment of the costs should be made. See **5.7** for further comment on calculating the proportion of expenditure that can qualify.

Expenses

The legislation states that in the following circumstances expenses can be treated as staffing costs:

> "...an amount paid by the company to a director or an employee of the company, other than an amount paid in respect of benefits in kind, if—
>
> (a) the amount is paid in respect of expenses paid by the director or employee, and
>
> (b) the amount is paid because of the director's or employee's employment."

HMRC have changed their guidance on the application of this over time. Currently, HMRC's position is that expenses which are incurred by the individual and reimbursed by the company can potentially qualify. This is subject to restrictions and HMRC have given detailed guidance on their position. This position is a less restrictive view than has been given in the past but it is important to consider the current guidance in the light of the wording of the legislation.

HMRC guidance states that reimbursements may qualify as staff cost where:

- the expense constitutes an expense to the company of employing staff, and
- the expense is an expense the employee pays in order to fulfil the requirements of her employment.

HMRC specifically highlight travel and subsistence expenses as being potentially qualifying. However, HMRC state the view that home to work travel and reimbursed training costs cannot qualify.

Detailed examples setting out HMRC's view are found at CIRD 83200.

Law: CTA 2009, s. 1123, 1124
Guidance: CIRD 83200

5.4.4 Software and consumable items

The following costs qualify under this category:

- computer software;
- consumable items or transformable materials.

New rules apply to consumable items and transformable materials which are sold. Comment on this is included below.

Software

Expenditure on computer software used within the R&D project can be included within an R&D claim. Care should be taken to include only non-capital expenditure on computer software licences, not capital costs on the purchase of software products.

On occasion a company will develop bespoke computer software for use within an existing R&D project; this could qualify as an R&D project in its own right.

Where these items are not used directly in the relevant R&D, an appropriate proportion of the costs should be taken.

Consumable items and transformable stores

Items which are consumed or transformed as part of the R&D work can be qualifying expenditure. There is no conclusive definition of this in the legislation but it specifically includes water, fuel and power.

Guidance on HMRC's interpretation of the terms "consumed" and "transformed" is given at CIRD 82400. All categories of expenditure on the R&D project should be considered when deciding what to claim but in HMRC's view the key element in deciding whether an asset is consumed or transformed is that it is either:

- used up in the R&D; or
- changed in such a way as it is no longer usable in its original form.

Where these items are not used directly in the relevant R&D, an appropriate proportion of the costs should be taken. Where an exact allocation cannot be ascertained, it is possible to claim a broad apportionment. For example, an apportionment based on head count could be taken for light and heating costs in an open plan office used for both R&D and non R&D activities.

The cost of the development of prototypes can take up a large proportion of the costs of developing a new product. The R&D tax relief on these costs can be significant and so should be analysed carefully. See below for more detailed comment on prototypes.

Consumable items sold

For expenditure incurred from 1 April 2015 onwards, new rules were introduced restricting the relief on consumable items which form part of the item produced which is transferred, for example a "first in class" piece of machinery.

Expenditure which meets all of the following criteria is not treated as attributable to relevant R&D, and so no longer qualifies.

For an item produced:

- the relevant R&D relates to an item which is produced in the course of the R&D;
- the consumable items form part of the item produced;
- the item is transferred by a "relevant person" (see below) for consideration in money or money's worth; and
- the transfer is made in the ordinary course of the relevant person's business.

For a process the following criteria apply:

- the relevant R&D relates to a process of producing an item;
- the consumable items form part of the item produced in the course of that R&D;
- the item is transferred by a relevant person for consideration in money or money's worth; and
- the transfer is made in the ordinary course of the relevant person's business.

Where only part of the item (or items) is transferred then an appropriate proportion of the qualifying costs are treated as not attributable to R&D.

A transfer will usually be by way of sale but this can also include the hiring out or letting of the item.

Relevant person

A "relevant person" is widely defined and covers companies and persons contracting with the claimant as well as the claimant itself. A relevant person can be any of the following:

- the company incurring the cost;
- the company to which the R&D is contracted out;
- the person (other than a company) who contracts out the R&D to a company and incurs the cost of the R&D;
- the person (other than a company) to whom the R&D is contracted out; or
- a person who is connected to a company or person in the above categories (see **5.4.2** above for the definition of connection).

Law: CTA 2009, s. 1125-1126B
Guidance: CIRD 82300-82400

5.4.5 Externally provided workers

Where a company, SME or large, makes a payment to an external staff provider for the provision of staff, the payment ("staff provision payment") can qualify for R&D relief. These rules can apply to staff provided by employment agencies and to staff provided by other companies within a group. The rules are very prescriptive and care should be taken with contractual arrangements to ensure that all of the conditions are met.

All of the following conditions must be met to qualify as an externally provided worker ("EPW").

- Condition A – the EPW is an individual (not a company).
- Condition B – the EPW is not a director or employee of the claimant company.
- Condition C – the EPW must personally provide, or is under an obligation personally to provide, services to the claimant company.
- Condition D – the EPW is subject to (or to the right of) supervision, direction or control by the claimant company as to the manner in which those services are provided.

- Condition E – the services are supplied to the claimant company through a staff provider ("SP").
- Condition F – the EPW provides, or is under an obligation to provide, those services personally to the claimant company under the terms of a contract with a person other than the claimant company (the staff controller ("SC")).
- Condition G – the provision of those services does not constitute the carrying on of activities contracted out by the claimant company.

An entity can be both a staff provider and a staff controller.

All of these conditions must be met for a payment to be treated as made for EPWs. The contractual arrangements should be reviewed in detail to ensure that they meet all of the tests.

Law: CTA 2009, s. 1127-1132

Benefit

Where the company is not connected to both the staff provider and the staff controller, qualifying expenditure is 65% of the payments made to the staff provider. The reduction is to remove the profit element made by the staff provider.

Where the company and both the staff provider and the staff controller are connected, the company does not claim a proportion of its expenditure but the whole payment or, if lower, the cost of provision of the staff controller (the SC's "relevant expenditure"). The staff provision payment must be included in the profits of the staff provider's accounts for a period of account ending not more than a year after the end of the accounting period of the claimant company in which the staff provision payment was included. In addition, the SC's relevant expenditure must:

- be included in the SC's accounts for a period ending not more than a year after the end of the accounting period of the claimant company in which the staff provision payment was included;
- be incurred by the SC in providing for the company the EPW;

- not be capital; and
- be on staffing costs or on paying agency workers.

An election can be made jointly by the company, the SP and SC to be treated as though they were connected. This could be beneficial where the cost to the SC is greater than 65% of the staff provision payment. However, this election would require the SP and SC to disclose their profit margin to the company, which is clearly sensitive in practice.

Contractual arrangements

Historically, the concept of an SC was not included in the legislation. The contract for provision of the services had to be between the worker and a staff provider. In effect there could only be three parties involved in the arrangement (a tripartite agreement including the claimant company).

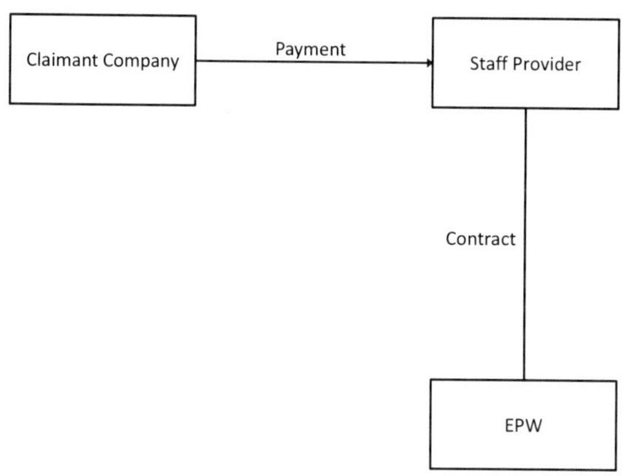

The concept of SC was introduced and the contract for services could now be with any person other than the claimant company. So now the supply chain can have any number of parties.

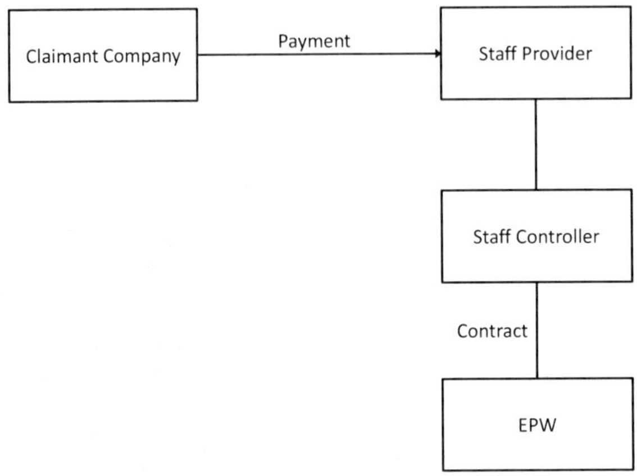

5.4.6 *Relevant clinical trials*

This category applies primarily to the pharmaceutical industry. Payments made to the subjects of clinical trials can be qualifying expenditure for R&D tax reliefs. A clinical trial is defined specifically as "an investigation in human subjects undertaken in connection with the development of a health care treatment or procedure".

Law: CTA 2009, s. 1140

5.5 Qualifying expenditure – SME only

5.5.1 *Subcontracted R&D*

Where an SME subcontracts part of the relevant R&D to another party the related cost can qualify for the R&D relief. See **4.10.5** for more detail on the definition of subcontracted R&D.

Importantly the work carried out by the subcontractor does not need to be R&D from the perspective of the subcontractor. The work undertaken by the subcontractor can be routine for them as long as it represents qualifying R&D work for the claimant company.

Law: CTA 2009, s. 1133-1136

Benefit

As is the case for externally provided workers, the qualifying expenditure is 65% of the payments made to the subcontractor where the claimant company and the subcontractor are not connected.

Where the company and the subcontractor are connected, the company does not claim a proportion of its expenditure but the full payment to the subcontractor or, if lower, the cost of provision to the subcontractor ("the subcontractor's relevant expenditure"). The subcontractor payment and the subcontractor's relevant expenditure must be included when calculating the profits in the subcontractor's accounts for a period of account ending not more than a year after the end of the accounting period of the claimant company. The subcontractor's relevant expenditure:

- must be incurred in the carrying on of the R&D activities, for the claimant company;
- must not be capital in nature;
- must consist of payments for one of the following:
  - staffing costs;
  - software or consumable items;
  - relevant payments to the subjects of clinical trials; or
  - externally provided workers; and
- must not be subsidised (see **4.10.3**).

An election can be made jointly by the company and the subcontractor to be treated as though they were connected. This could be beneficial where the cost to the subcontractor is greater than 65% of the subcontracting payment. However, this election would require the subcontractor to disclose its profit margin to the principal, which is usually commercially sensitive.

5.6 Qualifying expenditure – RDEC scheme

5.6.1 Introduction

The rules for certain types of expenditure differ between the SME scheme and the RDEC scheme (including the RDEC scheme for SMEs). Detailed rules on the particular qualifying requirements are included in **Chapters 6 and 7**. Below is a summary of the rules relating to subcontracted R&D for those not claiming under the SME scheme and contributions made for independent research.

5.6.2 R&D contracted out by the claimant

The rules for claiming costs which are contracted out are far more restrictive than under the SME scheme. Where a company claiming under the RDEC scheme contracts out activities, it is possible to claim R&D relief if the payment is made to:

- a qualifying body;
- an individual; or
- a firm, each member of which is an individual.

There are further conditions to meet which differ depending on the scheme the company is claiming under. These are covered in detail in **Chapters 6** and **7**.

5.6.3 Contributions to independent research

This type of expenditure is available to *large companies only* (so not to SMEs, even if claiming under the RDEC scheme for SMEs). To qualify, the following conditions should be met:

- the payment must be made to one of the following for the purpose of funding the R&D carried on by that party:
  - a qualifying body;
  - an individual; or
  - a firm, each member of which is an individual.
- the funded R&D must be attributable to relevant R&D (see **3.3**) of the company making the contribution;
- the funded R&D must not be contracted out to the funded body by another person;
- (if funding an individual) the large company must not be connected with the individual when the payment is made; and
- (if funding a firm other than a qualifying body) the large company is not connected with any member of the firm when the payment is made.

Law: CTA 2009, s. 104L, 104Y

Qualifying body

The following could be qualifying bodies:

- a charity;
- an institution of higher education;
- a scientific research organisation; or
- a health service body.

CTA 2009, s. 1142 sets out details of the particular conditions for the above categories.

Other bodies can be designated as qualifying bodies by the Treasury. This includes overseas bodies which are similar in nature to the above bodies. CIRD 82250 sets out the overseas bodies currently designated as qualifying bodies. This has been updated to include recent amendments made by *The Research and Development (Qualifying Bodies)(Tax) Order* 2018.

Law: CTA 2009, s. 1142; SI 2018/217
Guidance: CIRD 82250

5.7 How much cost will qualify?

5.7.1 Introduction

Where expenditure is not fully on R&D an apportionment should be made. This is particularly relevant to staffing costs as most employees will undertake some activities which are not treated as R&D for tax purposes. There is guidance on the extent of R&D projects in the BEIS guidelines.

To qualify as R&D for tax purposes activities must either:

- directly contribute to the project; or
- be treated as qualifying indirect activities.

5.7.2 Expenditure directly contributing to R&D

Activities directly contribute to an advance in science or technology if they "attempt to resolve an element of the scientific or technological uncertainty associated with achieving the advance."

The BEIS guidelines (at para. 27) pick out certain activities which are said to contribute directly to the advance.

> "Activities which directly contribute to R&D include:
>
> (a) activities to create or adapt software, materials or equipment needed to resolve the scientific or technological uncertainty, provided that the software, material or equipment is created or adapted solely for use in R&D;
>
> (b) scientific or technological planning activities; and
>
> (c) scientific or technological design, testing and analysis undertaken to resolve the scientific or technological uncertainty."

This list should not be seen as exhaustive but simply as providing examples of what could qualify. See below for further discussion on R&D planning activities.

5.7.3 Qualifying indirect activities

Certain activities which do not "directly contribute" to the R&D can qualify. These "qualifying indirect activities" ("QIAs") are set out specifically in the BEIS guidelines (at para. 31, reproduced here):

> "These are activities which form part of a project but do not directly contribute to the resolution of the scientific or technological uncertainty. They are:
>
> (a) scientific and technical information services, insofar as they are conducted for the purpose of R&D support (such as the preparation of the original report of R&D findings);
>
> (b) indirect supporting activities such as maintenance, security, administration and clerical activities, and finance and personnel activities, insofar as undertaken for R&D;
>
> (c) ancillary activities essential to the undertaking of R&D (e.g. taking on and paying staff, leasing laboratories and maintaining research and development equipment including computers used for R&D purposes);
>
> (d) training required to directly support an R&D project;

(e) research by students and researchers carried out at universities;

(f) research (including related data collection) to devise new scientific or technological testing, survey, or sampling methods, where this research is not R&D in its own right; and

(g) feasibility studies to inform the strategic direction of a specific R&D activity."

Activities which do not directly contribute and do not fall within one of these categories are not treated as R&D for tax purposes.

5.7.4 Start and end of R&D

When calculating the proportion of expenditure which qualifies for R&D, it is important to define carefully the start and end of a project.

Start of R&D (and planning as R&D)

The BEIS guidelines (at para. 33) state that R&D "...begins when work to resolve the scientific or technological uncertainty starts".

This means that defining the scientific or technological uncertainty as carefully as possible will help to maximise the value of the claim. Care should be taken to include the work involved in the initial planning stage of the project as these activities often involve senior members of staff and considerable cost.

Planning activities can "directly contribute" to the R&D project. The BEIS guidelines (at para. 36) give the following examples of activities which may directly contribute to the R&D:

> "Scientific or technological planning activities associated with a project directly contribute to resolving the scientific or technological uncertainty associated with the project, and are therefore R&D. These include defining scientific or technological objectives, assessing scientific or technological feasibility, identifying particular scientific or technological uncertainties, estimating development time, schedule, and resources of the R&D, and high-level outlining of the scientific or technical work, as well as the detailed planning and management of the work."

End of R&D

The qualifying R&D project ends when the scientific or technological uncertainty is resolved (or work to resolve it ceases). The BEIS guidelines (at para. 34) state that this occurs when:

> "knowledge is codified in a form usable by a competent professional working in the field, or when a prototype or pilot plant with all the functional characteristics of the final process, material, device, product or service is produced."

Where an R&D project has finished the position should be analysed as to whether any new uncertainties have arisen, meaning that the project is extended, or whether a new project has started.

Prototypes

A "prototype" is defined by the BEIS guidelines (at para. 39) as:

> "an original model on which something new or appreciably improved is patterned, and of which all things of the same type are representations or copies. It is a basic experimental model possessing the essential characteristics of the intended process, material, device, product or service."

The Guidelines also make the following comment on when the costs of the prototype cease to be R&D:

> "Once any modifications necessary to reflect the test findings have been made to the prototypes, and further testing has been satisfactorily completed, the scientific or technological uncertainty has been resolved and further work will not be R&D."

Expenditure on prototypes, especially when the prototypes are sold, is a complex area which has been a focus of HMRC. Care should be taken to review carefully the costs which can qualify. In particular, attention should be paid to the rules explained at **5.4.4** above (under "Consumable items sold") when considering this point. Evidence of the technological uncertainty will be important in successfully arguing that this type of cost qualifies for the relief.

5.7.5 Design and cosmetic and aesthetic effects

Work on the appearance of a product does not generally qualify as R&D work. For example, if a company is developing an enhanced sensor device and spends time in redesigning the external appearance of the casing as part of the wider R&D project this would not necessarily be treated as R&D. But the fact that the end result of the R&D work is aesthetic or cosmetic does not mean the work in producing this result is not R&D where the effect was created using science or technology. For example, work to create new software to produce an improved visual effect for a computer game could qualify.

Guidance: BEIS guidelines, para. 42

6. Large RDEC scheme

6.1 Introduction

Whilst the RDEC scheme is not as beneficial as the SME scheme, significant benefits can still be gained as the overall spend is often much higher. The greater part of the total tax relief given under the R&D scheme is under the RDEC scheme, even though the SME scheme makes up the majority of the claims.

On 1 April 2013 the most significant changes to the R&D expenditure reliefs came into effect since the introduction of the "large super-deduction scheme" in 2002. Since this date, large companies (and companies claiming under the large scheme for SMEs) have been able to claim the RDEC. This tax relief is treated as income in the accounts of the company and is included in the profit before tax, which is why it was originally referred to as the "above the line credit". This change was intended to:

- increase the prominence of the relief in the accounts;
- allow the relief to be more easily included in departmental budgeting;
- allow large loss making companies immediate benefit from making a claim; and
- increase the benefit for certain large international groups.

For the first few years of the RDEC there was some flexibility regarding which relief can be chosen. Until 1 April 2016, a company could decide whether to claim under the large super-deduction scheme or the RDEC.

If no election under the RDEC has been made, the company could continue to make claims under the large scheme until 31 March 2016. If the company claimed under the RDEC it could no longer make claims under the large scheme.

For expenditure from 1 April 2016 it is no longer possible to claim under the "super-deduction" large scheme. The cash benefit of the super-deduction relief is lower than relief under the RDEC scheme so a claim under the RDEC scheme is more beneficial during the period the schemes ran concurrently. Although, theoretically, claims could be made under the super-deduction scheme for large companies, this aspect is not covered in detail in this book due to the higher benefit of the RDEC scheme.

This chapter covers the RDEC scheme for large companies. SME entities can claim under the RDEC scheme in certain circumstances, and this is covered in **Chapter 7**.

Law: CTA 2009, Pt. 3, Ch. 6A

6.2 Rate of relief

The headline rate of the RDEC is currently 12% of qualifying expenditure (increased from 11% with effect from 1 January 2018).

Unlike the other R&D schemes, the RDEC is subjected to tax at the company's marginal rate.

The following example is to illustrate the cash benefit of the scheme rather than the mechanism (see **6.3** for more complete examples).

Example

A Ltd is a large company with a year end of 31 March 2019. It incurs £500,000 of qualifying staff costs in the year.

Qualifying expenditure	£500,000
Gross RDEC at 12%	£60,000
Less tax at 19%	(£11,400)
Net benefit of RDEC	£48,600

The benefit is 9.72% of qualifying expenditure.

Law: CTA 2009, Pt. 3, Ch. 6A
Guidance: CIRD 89700

6.3 Calculation

6.3.1 Introduction

The current rate of the payable credit (from 1 January 2018) is 12% of the qualifying expenditure. The amount of RDEC to which the company is entitled is called the "set off amount". The set off amount must go through the following steps set out for the payment:

1. Offset against the corporation tax liability for the accounting period.
2. Any amount remaining after step 1 is reduced by notional tax at the main rate. The difference is termed the "step 2 amount" and is discussed below.
3. The set off amount is then reduced to the proportion of PAYE/NIC liability for the period relating to staff directly and actively engaged in the R&D (including externally provided workers provided to the claimant by other group companies).
4. The set off amount is then offset against corporation tax liabilities of the company for any other period.
5. Where an election is made, the set off amount can be surrendered to other group companies.
6. The set off amount is then offset against other amounts due to HMRC under or by virtue of any enactment or under a contract settlement.
7. The set off amount is then payable to the company subject to various restrictions (see **6.3.5**).

These steps are discussed below.

Example

A Ltd makes profits in the year to 31 March 2019 and has a tax liability in its draft tax computations of £38,000 before any R&D tax relief.

The profits chargeable to corporation tax are £200,000. Tax at 19% = £38,000.

A Ltd is a large company and identifies £100,000 of qualifying expenditure under the RDEC scheme. The company adjusts its draft accounts to include £12,000 of RDEC as income. The company's profits chargeable to corporation tax increase accordingly.

The profits chargeable to corporation tax are now £212,000. Tax at 19% = £40,280.

The set off amount is used to reduce the tax liability of the company.

Tax at 19%	£40,280
Less: set off amount	(£12,000)
Net amount due for payment	£28,280

The cash effect of the relief is to reduce the amount A Ltd is required to pay to HMRC by £9,720, or 9.72% of the qualifying spend.

Law: CTA 2009, s. 104M-104T

6.3.2 Step 2

Any amount remaining after step 1 is reduced by deducting a notional tax charge. The amount remaining after deducting the notional tax is termed the "net value of the set off amount". The difference between the amount after step 1 and the net value of the set off amount is termed the "step 2 amount" and is discussed below.

The net value of the set off amount is calculated by reducing the set off amount by the corporation tax which would have been charged on the RDEC at the main rate of corporation tax (excluding any amounts brought forward from prior periods as a result of step 3 below).

The step 2 amount can be carried forward and applied in discharging any corporation tax liability for any subsequent accounting period.

The step 2 amount can also be transferred to another group company. The definition of a group company for these purposes is the same as for group relief (see **6.7**). The surrender of the step 2 amount will not be treated as taxable income in the hands of the recipient and it will not be treated as a distribution.

Law: CTA 2009, s. 104N(3), 104O

6.3.3 Step 3

Broadly speaking, step 3 caps any RDEC repayment available at the amount of PAYE and NIC paid in respect of staff directly involved in the R&D (the "total expenditure on workers"). This can include staff of the company and externally provided workers (EPWs) provided by group companies.

Where any amount remaining after step 2 is greater than the "total expenditure on workers" for the accounting period, the amount of the set off amount is reduced to the level of the total expenditure on workers.

The reduction in the set off amount which results from step 3 can be carried forward and is treated as RDEC of the next accounting period.

Total expenditure on workers for an accounting period is the total of the following:

1. the company's relevant portion of staffing costs for the period; and
2. where the claimant is a member of a group (see **6.5**) and has incurred expenditure on externally provided workers (see **5.4.5**), the relevant portion of staffing costs for the period by the other group company in providing the workers.

For the purposes of (1) above, the relevant portion of staffing costs for an accounting period are costs that:

- are paid to, or in respect of, directors and employees of the claimant who are directly and actively engaged in relevant R&D of the claimant; and
- form part of the total amount of the company's PAYE and NIC liabilities for the accounting period.

The relevant portion of staffing costs of the group company (per (2) above) is calculated in the case of each worker as follows.

1. Calculate the amount of the expenditure that has been incurred by the group company in providing the EPW, has been incurred on staffing costs and forms part of the group company's PAYE and NIC liability for the accounting period.
2. Calculate the percentage using the formula (R/T) x 100, where:

- R is the amount of the company's qualifying expenditure on the EPW that has been taken into account when calculating the company's qualifying R&D expenditure for the period; and
- T is the total amount of the company's qualifying expenditure on the EPW.

3. Multiply the amount calculated in part 1 by the percentage in part 2.

The following are excluded when calculating a company's PAYE and NI liability:

- PAYE: ignore deductions for child and working tax credits;
- NIC: ignore deductions for statutory sick pay, statutory maternity pay, and child and working tax credits.

Where the payment period of the PAYE/NI does not fall wholly within the accounting period of the company, a just and reasonable apportionment between the two periods should be made.

Law: CTA 2009, s. 104P-104Q

6.3.4 Surrender to a group company

Under step 5 above, a company can elect to surrender the credit to another group company. The definition of a group for these purposes is the same as for group relief (see **6.7**).

The overlapping period is the period of time which is common to both companies' accounting periods.

The procedure for calculating the amount which can be surrendered is as follows:

1. first, calculate the amount of tax payable by the recipient for the "overlapping period";
2. next, calculate the amount of the credit relating to the overlapping period; and
3. finally, offset the amount given by step 2 against the amount given by step 1.

Example

B Ltd has a corporate tax liability for the year ended 31 December 2018.

C Ltd has an amount to surrender in respect of the year ended 31 March 2019.

The overlapping period is the period from 1 April 2018 to 31 December 2018.

Any amount left over relating to the period from 1 January 2019 to 31 March 2019 could be surrendered if B Ltd has a corporation tax liability for that period (in its accounting period to 31 December 2019).

The surrender of the credit will not be treated as taxable income in the hands of the recipient and it will not be treated as a distribution.

Law: CTA 2009, s. 104R

6.3.5 Step 7 – payable RDEC

Where a company has no corporate tax liability, it can claim a repayment from HMRC where any set off amount is left after the first six steps of the calculation process. The repayment is subject to certain restrictions and set-offs as covered below. To ensure that companies with no corporate tax liability do not receive a higher benefit than tax-paying companies the repayment is reduced by a notional tax charge at the main rate of tax for the relevant period (see step 2 at **6.3.2** above).

The repayment of the credit is reduced by any of the following liabilities to HMRC:

- corporation tax for any period (steps 1 and 4);
- PAYE/NIC for the payment dates within the period; or
- other amounts due to HMRC (step 6).

Where the company is not a going concern at the time of the claim, no amount will be repaid and the credit is extinguished. But if the company becomes a going concern before the deadline for making or amending a claim then the repayment should be made. This deadline is generally two years after the end of the accounting period in question. The definition of going concern is given at section 104T of CTA 2009 and is the same as for the SME scheme (see **4.10.1**).

If HMRC open an enquiry into the period, the amount does not need to be repaid until the enquiry is closed (although the Inspector has the discretion to make payments on a provisional basis).

Example

D Ltd makes profits in the year to 31 March 2019 but has a tax loss of £100,000 in its draft tax computations.

D Ltd is a large company and identifies £100,000 of qualifying expenditure under the RDEC scheme. The company adjusts its draft accounts to include £12,000 of RDEC as income (12% x £100,000). D Ltd pays £20,000 of PAYE and NIC in the period for employees directly and actively involved in the R&D (the "total expenditure on workers").

The set off amount of £12,000 is reduced to the net value of the set off amount (at step 2).

Set off amount after step 1	£12,000
Less step 2 amount (19%)	(£2,280)
Net value of the set off amount	£9,720

D Ltd has total expenditure on workers of £20,000, so the set off amount is not restricted by step 3.

D Ltd is a standalone company and has not made profits in previous periods and does not owe other monies to HMRC. At step 7, D Ltd claims a repayment of £9,720.

As a result of the RDEC claim, D Ltd's trade loss is reduced.

Loss for corporation tax before RDEC	£100,000
Less RDEC	£12,000
Loss after RDEC	£88,000

Although the losses are reduced, the set off amount of £2,280 is carried forward and can reduce the future corporate tax liability of the company. This reduces the tax liability rather than the profits chargeable to corporation tax. For example, if D Ltd has profits chargeable to corporation tax of £100,000 (after loss relief) and tax of £19,000 in the year to 31 March 2020, the step 2 amount will reduce the tax due to £16,720.

Law: CTA 2009, s. 104S-104T

6.4 Conditions

To qualify for the large RDEC scheme, the company must:

- be large throughout the period;
- carry on a trade; and
- have qualifying expenditure which is deductible against corporation tax of the company's trade for the accounting period (see below).

Finance (No. 2) Act 2015 introduced rules to exclude certain entities from claiming the RDEC. These entities are primarily institutes of higher education and charities. This exclusion applies for expenditure incurred on or after 1 August 2015.

Law: CTA 2009, s. 104A, 104WA

6.5 Qualifying expenditure

6.5.1 Overview

Qualifying expenditure under the large RDEC scheme falls into three categories:

1. R&D undertaken in-house;
2. R&D contracted out by the company; and
3. contributions to independent research.

Law: CTA 2009, s. 104J-104L

6.5.2 R&D undertaken in-house

Qualifying expenditure undertaken in-house must meet the following conditions:

- it falls into one of the following categories:
    - staff costs;
    - software or consumable items;

    - expenditure on externally provided workers; or
    - payments to the subjects of clinical trials.
- it is on R&D relevant for the company undertaken by the company itself (see **3.3**);
- if the R&D is contracted out to the company it is contracted to the company by either:
    - a large company; or
    - a person otherwise than in the course of carrying on a trade chargeable to corporation tax or income tax.

Law: CTA 2009, s. 104J

6.5.3 R&D contracted out by the company

Qualifying expenditure contracted out must meet the following conditions:

- the expenditure is on payments to the following where the work is undertaken by them (i.e. not subcontracted again):
    - a qualifying body,
    - an individual; or
    - a firm, each member of which is an individual;
- it is on R&D relevant for the company (see **3.3**);
- if the R&D is contracted out to the company it is contracted to the company by either:
    - a large company; or
    - a person otherwise than in the course of carrying on a trade chargeable to corporation tax or income tax.

Law: CTA 2009, s. 104K

6.5.4 Independent research

This is covered in detail at **5.6.3** above.

6.6 Refunds of qualifying expenditure

HMRC guidance states that for the RDEC scheme, refunds of contributions to independent research and subcontract payments will give rise to a clawback of the credit through a tax assessment.

Law: FA 1998, Sch. 18, para. 52(5)(aa)
Guidance: CIRD 89730

6.7 Group companies

The large RDEC scheme, and the RDEC scheme for SMEs, includes additional rules for group companies. These rules allow for R&D undertaken by another company within a group to be treated as relevant R&D for the claimant.

The rules for group companies can apply where:

- one group company (Company A in the diagram below) makes a payment to another company within the group (Company B in the diagram) in respect of activities contracted out from one to the other;
- if the work were to have been undertaken by A it would have been relevant R&D; and
- Companies A and B are in the same group at the time of the payment.

The rules mean that account is taken of the activities of Company A when deciding whether Company B is undertaking relevant R&D.

If Company B then contracts the R&D out to a third party, and the R&D is undertaken by the third party, then the R&D can be treated as being research contracted out by B.

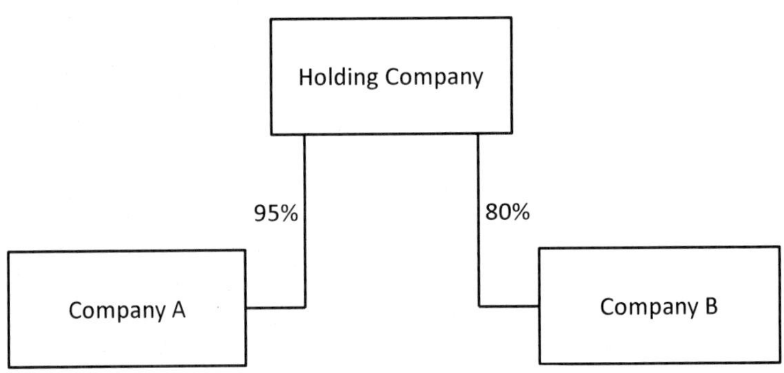

Law: CTA 2009, s. 104W

Group

Companies are treated as being in the same group if:

- one is a 75% subsidiary of another; or
- both are 75% subsidiaries of a third company.

A company is a 75% subsidiary of the parent if the parent:

- directly or indirectly beneficially owns at least 75% of its ordinary share capital;
- is beneficially entitled to at least 75% of the profits available for distribution; and
- is beneficially entitled to at least 75% of the assets available for distribution on a winding up.

Law: CTA 2010, Pt. 5, Ch. 5

7. RDEC scheme for SMEs

7.1 Introduction

There are three circumstances in which an SME may have to claim under the RDEC scheme for SMEs:

- R&D was subcontracted to the claimant ("subcontracted RDEC SME");
- expenditure is subsidised by another party ("subsidised RDEC SME");
- the cap for R&D expenditure has been exceeded ("capped RDEC SME").

It is possible for an SME to claim qualifying expenditure under any or all of the above, depending on the facts. The rules relating to the mechanism of relief (see **6.3**), exclusion of claims by charities and universities (see **6.4**), refunds of qualifying expenditure (see **6.6**) and group companies (see **6.7**) apply equally to the RDEC scheme for SMEs set out below.

Law: CTA 2009, Pt. 3, Ch. 6A

7.2 Subcontracted SME

7.2.1 Conditions

The company must:

- be carrying on a trade;
- be an SME in the accounting period;
- make qualifying expenditure on subcontracted R&D; and
- have qualifying expenditure which is deductible against corporation tax profits of the trade for the accounting period.

Law: CTA 2009, s. 104A

7.2.2 What is subcontracting?

Subcontracting is not defined in the legislation so must take its common usage. See **4.10.5** for guidance on the meaning.

7.2.3 Qualifying expenditure on subcontracted R&D

Qualifying expenditure under the subcontracted SME scheme falls into two categories:

- R&D undertaken in-house; and
- R&D contracted out by the company.

The expenditure must be incurred on R&D contracted out to the company by:

- a large company; or
- a person not carrying on a trade chargeable to corporation tax or income tax.

Law: CTA 2009, s. 104C

R&D undertaken in-house

Qualifying expenditure undertaken in-house must meet the following conditions:

- the R&D is undertaken by the company itself;
- it is on R&D relevant for the company (see **3.3**); and
- it falls into one of the following categories:
  - staff costs;
  - software or consumable items;
  - expenditure on externally provided workers; or
  - payments to the subject of clinical trials.

Law: CTA 2009, s. 104D

R&D contracted out by the company

Qualifying expenditure contracted out must meet the following conditions:

- the expenditure is on payments to the following where the work is undertaken by them (not subcontracted again):
  - a qualifying body,
  - an individual; or
  - a firm, each member of which is an individual;

- it is on R&D relevant for company (see **3.3**);

Law: CTA 2009, s. 104E

7.3 Subsidised SME

7.3.1 Introduction

A claim can be made under this scheme for expenditure made by an SME which does not fall within the SME scheme because it is subsidised (see **Chapter 4**).

Law: CTA 2009, Pt. 3, Ch. 6A

7.3.2 Conditions

The company must:

- carry on a trade;
- be an SME in the accounting period;
- make qualifying subsidised expenditure; and
- have qualifying expenditure which is deductible against corporation tax profits of the trade for the accounting period.

See **4.10.3** for guidance on the meaning of "subsidised expenditure".

Law: CTA 2009, s. 104A

7.3.3 Qualifying subsidised expenditure

Qualifying expenditure under the subsidised SMEs scheme falls into two categories:

- R&D undertaken in-house; and
- R&D contracted out by the company.

Law: CTA 2009, s. 104F

R&D undertaken in-house

Qualifying expenditure undertaken in-house must meet the following conditions:

- the expenditure is subsidised;
- it falls into one of the following categories:

  - staff costs;
  - software or consumable items;
  - expenditure on externally provided workers; or
  - payments to the subject of clinical trials;
- it is on R&D relevant for the company undertaken by the company itself (see **3.3**);
- the expenditure is not incurred by the company in carrying out activities contracted out to the company by any person.

Law: CTA 2009, s. 104G

R&D contracted out by the company

Qualifying expenditure contracted out must meet the following conditions:

- the expenditure is subsidised;
- the expenditure is on payments to the following where the work is undertaken by them (not subcontracted again):
  - a qualifying body;
  - an individual; or
  - a firm, each member of which is an individual;
- it is on R&D relevant for company (see **3.3**);
- the expenditure is not incurred by the company in carrying out activities contracted out to the company by any person.

Law: CTA 2009, s. 104H

7.4 Capped SME

7.4.1 Introduction

Where an SME company is restricted from making a claim under the SME scheme because the cap on R&D reliefs applies (see **Chapter 4**) then a claim can be made under the RDEC for SMEs.

7.4.2 Conditions

The company must:

- carry on a trade;

- be an SME in the accounting period; and
- have qualifying capped expenditure which is deductible against corporation tax profits of the trade for the accounting period.

Law: CTA 2009, s. 104A

Qualifying capped expenditure

Qualifying capped expenditure:

- cannot qualify for the SME scheme only because the expenditure is capped under CTA 2009 s. 1113 (see **4.10.2**);
- is not qualifying expenditure on subcontracted R&D; and
- would have been qualifying R&D expenditure had the company been large throughout the accounting period.

Law: CTA 2009, s. 104I

8. Practical steps – making the claim

8.1 Introduction

Firstly, and most importantly, a claim must be made in order to get the relief. If a company does not make a claim, or does not make a claim in time, then no R&D tax relief is due.

As the claim is made as part of the corporation tax return it is subject to the rules of "self-assessment". A company must complete a tax return (CT600) assessing its own corporate tax liability. The onus is on the company to decide how much R&D relief to claim and to include this on its self-assessment return. The service level taken on by HMRC is designed to reflect the importance of the credit to companies, especially SMEs. HMRC have the statutory right to enquire into the CT600 (see **8.3** below). The current guidance to Inspectors says that for SME claims 95% of R&D repayable credit claims should be repaid, or further queries raised, within 28 days of receipt of the claim. HMRC state that this only applies where the claim is made electronically and includes correct BACS details for the repayment. Where HMRC believe that the claim is incorrect then they state that they will open an enquiry within 60 days of receiving the claim.

To maximise the chances of a successful claim it is important to get the claim right first time; it should be carefully prepared and well presented. Published HMRC guidance comments that "arithmetic or typographic errors" are among the indications that a claim is higher risk.

It is advisable to present a full and complete case for the claim in the initial submission as this will maximise the chances of success and also give comfort about the success of a claim at an earlier date (see **8.3.3** on discovery assessments).

Law: FA 1998, Sch. 18

Guidance: CIRD 80530

8.2 Mechanism

8.2.1 Overview

The claim should be made as part of the submission of the company's corporation tax return. It can be made in the original return or as an amendment thereof. The submission must include the amount of the relief being claimed.

The deadline for making, amending or withdrawing an R&D tax relief claim is generally the first anniversary of the filing deadline for the tax return. The filing deadline for a corporation tax return is typically 12 months from the end of the accounting period. This usually means that a company will have two years from the end of the accounting period to file a revised tax return including a claim for the R&D relief. Care should always be taken to understand when the deadline falls. Detailed rules for the filing deadline are found in Sch. 18 of FA 1998.

8.2.2 Amending a tax return

Where a tax return has already been submitted it is possible to submit a revised return. This is important when looking to make a claim for the first time. Again, in these cases it is particularly important to pay attention to the deadline (as set out above).

Most returns and associated accounts have to be submitted online using the iXBRL protocol. Where the return has already been submitted with iXBRL "tagged accounts", the return can be re-submitted without re-attaching the tagged accounts.

8.2.3 Late claims

The deadline for submission of an R&D claim can be extended at HMRC's discretion. In general, late claims are not accepted other than in exceptional circumstances, where the reasons for not making the claim within the normal time limit are not in the claimant company's control. This treatment could apply where, for example, an officer of the company was absent due to illness.

The guidance specifically states that the following will not be treated as beyond the company's control:

- oversight or negligence;
- failure without good reason to compute the value of the claim; or
- illness or absence of an adviser.

Where an application to allow a late claim is made the following information should be sent to the Inspector:

- reasons why the claim is late;
- the extent to which it is late;
- consequences to the company if the claim is refused; and
- any unusual features of the claim which impacted on the timing of the submission.

This treatment is by concession and so, wherever possible, the claim should be made within the statutory limits.

Guidance: *Statement of Practice* 05/01

8.2.4 Deadline approaching

Where the deadline for filing the amended return is approaching the business should focus on calculating the qualifying expenditure figure and including this in the tax return. Although not ideal, it is possible to file the amended return without the detailed documentation of the claim and then to submit the detailed write up as soon as possible after the deadline.

8.2.5 Advance assurance

A new mechanism was introduced from November 2015 to allow small companies making a claim for the first time to get greater certainty that their R&D claim would be successful.

The "advance assurance" process may be helpful, though it is not obligatory as a company can simply file its claim as normal. The advantage of applying is that, where the R&D claim is in line with what was agreed during the advance assurance process, the company can be confident that the claims will be successful within the first three accounting periods.

The advance assurance process does not replace the filing of the claim as part of the corporation tax return. The claim must still be filed in the normal way.

The application is made online and the application will be followed up with a discussion with a member of HMRC's R&D specialist staff. It is advisable to get professional advice regarding the process and to assist with the application itself.

Following conclusion of the process, HMRC will issue a letter confirming whether the application has been successful.

HMRC may contact the company following the submission of the tax return to confirm that the claim matches the details provided as part of the advance assurance application.

In the 2017 Autumn Statement, HMRC announced that they plan to pilot a new advanced clearance service for RDEC claims.

Eligible companies

Eligible companies must:

- have a turnover not more than £2,000,000;
- have no more than 50 employees;
- be making a claim for the first time;
- where the company is part of a group, be the first company of the group to be making a claim;
- not have entered into a disclosable tax avoidance scheme;
- not be a "corporate serious defaulter".

What information is required

To make an advance assurance application you will need:

- company accounts;
- company registration documents;
- HMRC correspondence;
- previous company tax returns (where applicable);
- the name of an individual who will be dealing with the discussions regarding the application;
- detailed information on the R&D work.

8.3 Enquiries

8.3.1 Overview

HMRC have publicly stated that, if they feel that the claim is incorrect or incomplete, they should enquire into the return within 60 days. This does not supersede the rules relating to enquiries which are set out below. An Inspector can still enquire into the claim after the payment is made but this is not general practice as set out in the guidance given to Inspectors.

A company submits an R&D claim which is complete and correct to the best of its knowledge. HMRC then have a given period during which they can enquire into the corporation tax return, including the R&D tax relief claim. The detailed rules on how these enquiries are dealt with are outside the scope of this book but a brief discussion is included below to help the reader's understanding.

Typically, HMRC have one year from the date of the submission of the return to enquire into the corporation tax return of a company. For companies which are not small (as defined by the *Companies Act* 2006), the period is extended to the first anniversary of the filing date of the corporation tax return. If a return is filed late, then the period in which an enquiry can be open is extended.

8.3.2 Enquiry period for amended returns

Where a company amends the corporation tax return after it has been filed, the enquiry period is extended, though in principle the period is only extended for the element of the return that has been amended. In most circumstances, therefore, if the R&D element is the only part of the return that has been amended the Inspector can only enquire into the R&D claim itself once the normal enquiry period has come to an end.

8.3.3 Discovery assessments

Once the period for an enquiry has passed, or the enquiry has closed, HMRC must open a discovery assessment to be able to review the return. A discovery assessment can only be raised in certain specific circumstances, where:

- the situation giving rise to the under-assessment arose from "careless" or "deliberate" actions of the claimant or its agent; or
- the Inspector could not reasonably be expected to have been aware of the situation giving rise to the under-assessment based on the information made available to him.

To minimise the possibility of a discovery assessment being raised the company should provide sufficient information in the returns or computations to allow the Inspector to evaluate the claim properly. For this reason, and to expedite the cash payment, it is advisable to include disclosure of the specifics of how the tests for the reliefs were met.

The person reading the claim is unlikely to be an expert in the field of science or technology to which the claim relates. For this reason it is important to ensure that any information provided is in plain English and, where necessary, an explanation of the relevant technical terms is given.

HMRC's Inspectors will usually attempt to deal with any minor queries about the claim informally, i.e. without opening a formal statutory enquiry. This approach is usually beneficial to both parties and allows queries to be dealt with quickly and with little interruption to the claimant's business. Where an agreement cannot be reached using this approach the Inspector may seek to open a formal enquiry. Care should be taken when entering into informal discussions with HMRC. It should be noted that where a formal enquiry has not been opened into the tax return, the rules which apply to such enquiries do not apply.

8.4 HMRC approach

8.4.1 Introduction

HMRC publish their guidance to Inspectors on how to review R&D tax relief claims. Below is a summary of the key areas they will consider in reviewing a claim:

- what was the advance in science or technology that was being sought?

- what was the R&D project, and (if relevant) what was the larger commercial project?
- what were the particular scientific or technological uncertainties that needed to be resolved to seek the advance?
- in what way does the project go beyond the current state of knowledge?
- why was the knowledge or capability sought not readily deducible by a competent professional in the field?
- when were the particular uncertainties overcome?
- what activities within the project fall within the statutory definition of R&D for tax purposes?

It would be advisable to include information in answer to these questions in the original claim.

Guidance: CIRD 80520

8.4.2 Risk factors

HMRC approach a claim using a risk based approach, focusing resources on areas of higher risk. Particular risk factors highlighted by HMRC (adapting the guidance at CIRD 80530) include:

- a lack of analysis of why the relief is due;
- simple arithmetic or typographic errors;
- the trade of the company, as HMRC consider that certain trades are less likely to involve R&D; and
- the solvency position of the company, as it is harder to recover any relief paid to an insolvent company.

8.4.3 Common errors

HMRC guidance sets out various "common errors" which are useful to note and to avoid in the presentation of the claim. The following list is based on guidance at CIRD 80540, but references to the relevant chapters of this book have been added for easy reference:

- companies making a claim under the wrong scheme (see **Chapter 4**);

- claims made for certain activities of the project which are not R&D (see **Chapter 2**);
- claims made for expenditure which does not qualify for the relief (see **Chapter 5**), in particular:
  - claims for staffing costs for individuals who are not employees or directors; or
  - claims for overheads which do not qualify;
- failure to apply the rules for connected parties (see **5.4.2**);
- for the tax credit the common errors include:
  - failure to apply the restriction of the surrenderable loss to the super-deduction (see **5.2.2**); and
  - carrying forward the loss rather than surrendering it;
- claiming under the SME scheme for subsidised R&D (see Section **4.10.3**).

8.5 Record keeping

A company is subject to general record keeping requirements and, in addition, there is some guidance given by HMRC which is specific to R&D claims. There are, however, no specific requirements for R&D. It is useful to open a dialogue with the Inspector to discuss the types of document which could be given but also to consider the reasonableness of any request.

It is important to collect and keep documentation relating to the R&D projects and to evidence a systematic, well documented approach when dealing with enquiries from HMRC. HMRC do accept that larger organisations with a track record of R&D work are likely to have more detailed records than a smaller company working on its first project, and they should tailor their requests for information to reflect this.

A robust, on-going process throughout the period of the project will make the preparation of the claim after the year end far easier. The problems and uncertainties of the project are easier to recall and to explain when they are fresh in the mind rather than a couple of years later.

8.6 Optimising documentation

8.6.1 Planning material

If beginning a new project, it is advisable to consider how the documentation could reflect the systematic approach the company is taking and give contemporaneous evidence of how the scientific or technological advancement and scientific or technological uncertainty are being viewed.

HMRC suggest the following may be included in project planning materials to document the R&D process:

"• What the R&D aim of the project is – i.e. what advance in science or technology is being sought. This would be expected to include references to the current state of knowledge and/or technology and indicate what scientific or technological hurdles have to be overcome to achieve the desired advance.

- A link between the outcome of the R&D project and its effect on the commercial prospects for the company – In order to meet the relevant to the trade tests (CIRD81400) one would expect to see the R&D project (or the larger commercial project in which it is embedded) considered in terms of its benefit to the company.
- A review of the current state of knowledge – One cannot be prescriptive about what form this would take but it might include any patent searches, reviews of the scientific or technological aspects of competitor products, and trade journal or scientific articles which indicate the state of knowledge and advancement in the particular sector, technology or trade.
- What difficulties are foreseen for the project – This would include a review of the scientific or technological uncertainties (not just 'we don't know if it could work' but an indication of the specific areas of scientific or technological uncertainty that would have to be resolved in the context of the current state of scientific or technological knowledge in the field).

- A structure for the project setting out the activities, who will undertake them, and what the stages are that need to be achieved to get the desired result.
- Notes on the particular expertise specific employees, consultants or subcontractors will bring to the project, why they have been selected and what they are expected to do."

Guidance: CIRD 80560

8.6.2 Ongoing records

Ideally the company will already be monitoring and recording the progress of the project which will help to record how it progressed and evolved over time. HMRC guidance on this reads as follows:

> "As the project develops you may also find:
>
> - notes on how the uncertainties and other challenges were overcome (or not),
> - information about any major changes to the aims, or new uncertainties that have been encountered,
> - details of any patent applications filed, or how any resultant, identified intellectual property is to be protected,
> - internal progress reports."

Timesheet records (also covered below) can be a powerful tool for documenting R&D activity. They are contemporaneous to the work and show a strong link to the work undertaken. Ideally the individuals submitting the timesheets should have an understanding of how to categorise and record their work in terms of R&D tax reliefs.

Many companies simply do not use timesheets in the business and where this is the case it is important to include how much time is being spent on the project in ongoing project documentation.

Guidance: CIRD 80560

8.6.3 Expense records

HMRC state that they do not expect reference to underlying records to be part of all enquiries but may require some evidence of the expenses paid. A company should consider the reasonableness of any request for underlying documentation. Where appropriate it may be reasonable to suggest sampling of records rather than a review of all cases.

HMRC have highlighted the following examples. This is an extensive list but the guidance (at CIRD 80570) states that these lists "are indicative not mandatory, but they may be helpful in deciding what evidence there is and what it may be helpful to review in order to consider particular points." Bold has been added below for greater clarity.

> **"Contributions to independent research (large companies only) CIRD82200**
>
> - Copies of notes of meetings or correspondence relating to the research and why it is considered to be relevant to the trade.
> - Copies of any agreements or contracts relating to the contribution.
> - Evidence the contributions were paid, such as bank records.
>
> **Software CIRD82500**
>
> - Receipts or contracts for software purchased, licensed or commissioned.
> - A copy of product/marketing literature for the software if it is necessary to demonstrate what it is used for.
> - Any evidence – e.g. internal cost accounting codes – showing it was properly charged to the R&D activity.
>
> **Staffing costs CIRD83000**
>
> - PAYE records.
> - Records of pension payments.
> - List of R&D staff.
> - R&D staff's timesheets (for those not full time on the project).
> - Contracts of employment for R&D staff.

Externally provided workers CIRD84000

- Documentary evidence of the contract or arrangement with the staff provider.
- Copy of invoices received.
- Evidence of payments – e.g. bank records.
- Details of the activities carried out and any evidence of active supervision by the company.

Subcontract costs CIRD84200

- Invoices from subcontractors.
- Evidence of the nature of the work subcontracted and the terms applicable. We would generally expect there to be a written contract or evidence of the terms of the agreement.
- Evidence of payments – e.g. bank records."

9. R&D capital allowances

9.1 Introduction

The R&D tax relief cannot be claimed for capital assets (see section **3.4.3**) which are specifically excluded from relief under the R&D expenditure reliefs (set out in **Chapters 5 to 7**).

Capital assets are essential to many R&D projects and the costs of these can be significant, for example the purchase of computers, testing equipment and laboratories. This has been recognised and a special regime of allowances, which give better tax relief for these assets, has been put in place. These enhanced "research and development allowances" (RDAs), are discussed below. In certain cases, such as on the acquisition of buildings, RDAs give tax relief where previously relatively little relief may otherwise have been available. This could give rise to significant savings to claimants, especially for the buildings which are to be used wholly for R&D purposes. From October 2018, however, new tax reliefs for buildings were introduced with the new structures and buildings allowances (the detailed rules for which are under consultation at the time of writing).

General tax relief for the costs of purchasing tangible capital assets is given by way of capital allowances. These have been described as the tax equivalent of deprecation, but the law sets different rates of tax relief for expenditure on different types of asset. For plant and machinery, for example, the general rate of allowance is currently 18% per year but the rate can be as low as 6% for certain types of plant. Furthermore, plant and machinery allowances are calculated on the reducing balance each year. RDA assets, by contrast, attract 100% allowances in year one, and can therefore significantly accelerate the receipt of tax relief for the assets in question.

The use of the annual investment allowance ("AIA"), available for most expenditure on plant or machinery, should be considered in conjunction with consideration of RDAs. The AIA gives 100% relief in the first year for certain expenditure. The AIA is subject to a limit, which is currently (from 1 January 2019) £1,000,000 per annum.

A detailed analysis of the capital allowances rules is outside the scope of this book. See, however, *Capital Allowances* 2019-20, also published by Claritax Books (which now also includes a substantial chapter on the structures and buildings allowance).

The chart below illustrates the cumulative tax relief for an asset costing £100,000 over the first 10 years of its life (where the AIA is not available, and where allowances are given at 18% or the lower historic rate of 8%).

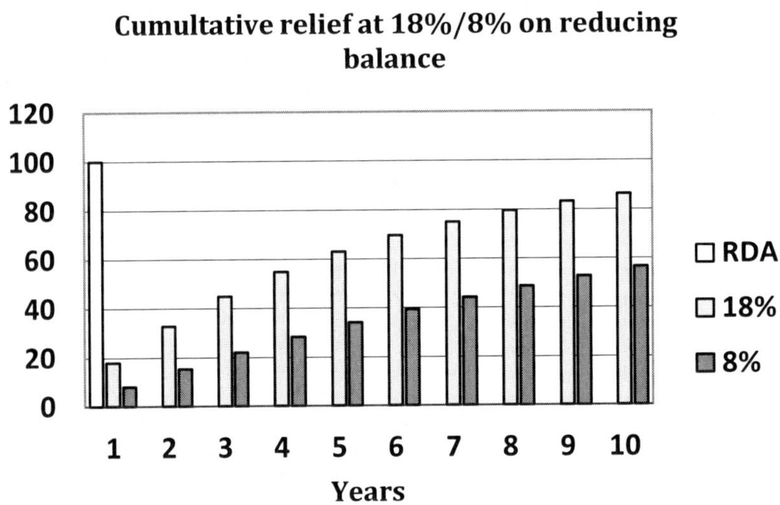

9.2 Summary of qualifying criteria

The R&D allowance for capital expenditure is not solely for companies but can also be claimed by individuals and partnerships. The focus in this chapter, however, is for companies.

The key questions to ask when deciding whether to make a claim are:

- is the company undertaking R&D?
- is the expenditure on an R&D asset?
- is the capital expenditure qualifying expenditure?

Each of these is considered in turn below.

Law: CAA 2001, Pt. 6

9.3 Is the company undertaking R&D for RDA purposes?

The definition of R&D for RDA purposes is based on the definition under GAAP and the BEIS guidelines. The expenditure must be capable of being treated as R&D under GAAP, but there is no requirement that the accounts explicitly refer to the R&D. The work does not need to be capitalised as R&D in the accounts. The activities undertaken should also be treated as R&D under the BEIS guidelines.

In contrast to R&D expenditure reliefs, R&D for RDA purposes is extended to include oil and gas exploration and appraisal.

Law: CAA 2001, s. 437

9.4 Is the expenditure on R&D?

9.4.1 Introduction

Having established that the company is undertaking R&D it is essential that the capital expenditure must be on R&D. This includes expenditure on:

- carrying out the R&D; or
- the provision of facilities for carrying out the R&D.

Expenditure on purchasing rights in R&D, or rights arising out of R&D, does not qualify.

Examples given by HMRC of qualifying expenditure include a laboratory in which a taxpayer intends to carry out R&D and a car used by an employee to travel around different R&D sites.

Guidance: CA 60300

9.4.2 Dwellings

It is possible to include "dwellings" within a claim but certain criteria must be met to do so.

Dwellings are initially excluded from the relief but can qualify if both:

- the dwelling is part of a building which is otherwise used for R&D; and

- no more than 25% of the expenditure on the complete building relates to the dwelling.

Where both conditions are met, the whole of the cost of the building could qualify for RDAs. Otherwise, the proportion of the cost relating to the dwelling must be excluded from the claim.

Example 1

A Ltd builds a laboratory which costs £10 million, which includes £2 million of capital expenditure on dwellings for technical staff within the building.

In this case, all of the costs qualify for RDAs.

Example 2

B Ltd builds a laboratory which costs £10 million, which includes £3 million of capital expenditure on dwellings for technical staff within the building.

In this case, £7 million of the cost will qualify for RDAs.

Law: CAA 2001, s. 438

9.5 Is the expenditure "qualifying expenditure"?

9.5.1 Overview

The legislation sets out the types of expenditure that qualify for the relief. Where the expenditure only partly meets this test then a "just and reasonable apportionment" between qualifying expenditure and non-qualifying expenditure should be made.

To be able to claim the relief the expenditure must be incurred on R&D directly undertaken by the company or on the company's behalf. This will be the case if:

- the company is carrying on a trade when the expenditure is incurred and the R&D relates to that trade; or
- after incurring the expenditure, the company commences a trade connected to the R&D.

CAA 2001, s. 439A sets out special rules applicable to Northern Ireland establishments.

9.5.2 Related to the trade

The expenditure must be related to the company's trade. Expenditure which is related to a trade includes expenditure which may lead to or facilitate an extension of the trade. It also specifically includes expenditure on medical research which is linked to the welfare of the company's employees working in the trade.

9.5.3 Land and buildings

Expenditure on the acquisition of land or rights over land is specifically excluded from the relief. Whilst the land itself cannot qualify, the expenditure on the buildings which are used in the R&D activity can. This can give rise to huge tax savings as tax relief on buildings will only otherwise be given for a proportion of the expenditure (i.e. to the extent that the costs are incurred on fixtures that qualify for plant and machinery allowances).

If expenditure is related to the acquisition of the following it could be included in a claim:

- building or structure already on the land;
- rights in or over such a building or structure; or
- plant and machinery which forms part of such a building or structure.

In addition, the construction of buildings (where unrelated to the acquisition of land) could also qualify.

Law: CAA 2001, s. 439-440

9.6 Mechanism

9.6.1 Introduction

For companies, RDAs are claimed as part of the corporation tax return (CT600). Broadly speaking, the RDA is treated as an expense of the trade to which it relates.

The RDA can be claimed at a rate of up to 100% of the qualifying expenditure. It is possible to reduce the claim below 100% but this is not generally advisable.

If the expenditure is incurred in periods before the company starts its trade, it is treated as being incurred in the year that the trade commences. This is a useful relaxation of the rules where companies have to incur expenditure in preparation for commencing their trade.

There are rules relating to VAT liabilities and rebates for R&D assets which are found in CAA 2001, Pt. 6, Ch. 4.

Law: CAA 2001, Pt. 6, Ch. 3

9.6.2 Cessation of ownership or demolition

An adjustment may be necessary where, after a company has claimed RDAs, it ceases to own the asset or the asset is demolished. A taxable receipt, giving rise to a "balancing charge", may arise in these circumstances. If the "disposal value" exceeds the tax written down value then a taxable receipt should be included when calculating the tax charge for the period. The taxable receipt is:

- the excess of disposal value over unclaimed RDA; or (if lower)
- the total RDA claimed.

This ensures that the taxable receipt does not claw back more than the original amount claimed.

Example 1

A Ltd builds a laboratory for £10 million in the year to 31 December 2012 and claims the full costs as RDA.

It disposes of the asset in the year ended 31 December 2018 for a sale value of £9 million. This sale value is the open market value of the asset.

In the year ended 31 December 2018 a charge of £9 million is included in the profits chargeable to tax of A Ltd.

Example 2

B Ltd purchases a laboratory for £10 million in the year to 31 December 2011 and claims the full costs as RDA.

It disposes of the asset in the year ended 31 December 2018 for a sale value of £11 million, being its market value at the time.

In the year ended 31 December 2018 a charge of £10 million is included in the profits chargeable to tax of B Ltd as the charge is limited to the original RDA claimed.

In the unlikely event that the disposal happens in the period in which the expenditure was incurred the RDA claimed is reduced by the "disposal value". Where the disposal value is equal to the RDA then it may be preferable not to claim the RDA at all.

Example 3

C Ltd builds a laboratory for a cost of £10 million in the year to 31 December 2018 and claims the full costs as RDA. It disposes of the asset in the same year for a disposal value of £9 million.

C Ltd will receive RDAs of £1 million (£10 million minus £9 million).

In the examples above, the companies would also need to consider tax adjustments for the accounting profit or loss on disposal of the asset and chargeable gains or losses.

9.6.3 Calculating the disposal value

The method of calculating the disposal value is determined by the circumstances of the disposal. The following table summarises this.

Disposal Event	Disposal Value
Sale of asset at not less than market value	Net sale proceeds
Demolition or destruction of the asset	Net amount received plus any insurance or other capital compensation
Otherwise	Market value of the asset at the time of the event

The use (in some circumstances) of market value is designed to stop companies avoiding or reducing a balancing charge by disposing of the asset for less than its worth, for example to a connected party.

If a company incurs demolition costs, these can be deducted from the disposal value in arriving at a balancing charge. It is possible for additional RDAs to be claimed at this point, if:

- the demolition costs exceed the disposal value; and
- the asset has not been used in an activity other than R&D before demolition.

The additional RDA would not arise, for example, if the R&D activity ceased and the building began to be used as a warehouse for storage.

10. Can a Patent Box claim be made?

10.1 Introduction

Since 1 April 2013, certain income derived from patents has been eligible for a reduced rate of corporation tax. This has been phased in with the full reduction, to a rate of just 10%. The 10% rate came into force from 1 April 2017.

The Patent Box is designed to work alongside the R&D tax reliefs to incentivise companies to keep their intellectual property in the UK after it is developed. There are specific rules which "carve out" the benefit from the R&D relief when calculating the Patent Box relief. This means that the benefit of the Patent Box is not reduced by a claim for R&D relief, and *vice versa*. The powerful combination of the R&D relief and the Patent Box can give cash back during the development phase and then provide a low tax rate once the company is making a profit.

The Patent Box came under scrutiny by various international bodies on the basis that it represents a harmful or unfair tax practice. The UK and German governments put together a joint proposal for the G20 and OECD in November 2014. This proposed the amendment of the existing Patent Box regime from June 2016 with its abolition in June 2021. It is proposed that a new regime based on a "Modified Nexus Approach" would replace the Patent Box. The rules were enacted in FA 2016 and these "new rules" generally apply for accounting periods beginning on or after 1 July 2016.

The benefit of the Patent Box is given by an additional deduction which is included in the corporation tax return. This means that the patent-related profits (called "relevant IP income") are effectively taxed at 10% (this was subject to transitional provisions below).

Law: CTA 2010, Pt. 8A

Guidance: https://www.gov.uk/government/uploads/system/uploads/attachment_ data/file/373135/GERMANY_UK_STATEMENT.pdf

10.2 How the benefit is calculated

The relief is given as an additional deduction in the corporation tax computation, rather than simply taxing the profits at the Patent Box rate. The additional deduction is calculated as follows:

RP x ((MR – IPR) / MR)

where:

RP = relevant IP profits

MR = main rate corporation tax

IPR = special IP rate of corporation tax (currently 10%)

Example

A Ltd has RP of £500,000 for the year ended 31 March 2019. At a 19% tax rate the tax payable on this amount would be £95,000.

The main rate of corporation tax for the year is 19% (MR) and the IP rate is 10% (IPR).

£500,000 x ((19-10)/19))

This gives an additional deduction of £236,842, which reduces the tax to £50,000 on the patent-related income:

Profits	£500,000
Less: Patent Box deduction	(£236,842)
Revised profit	£263,158

Corporation tax at 19% on the revised profit of £263,158 is £50,000, which represents an effective tax rate of 10% and a saving of £45,000 in tax terms.

Law: CTA 2010, s. 357A; Pt. 8A

Phasing in

The relief was phased in over four years from 1 April 2013, with the full relief available from 1 April 2017. Initially the relief is worth 60% of the final benefit. The phasing in of the relief was as follows:

Year ended	Proportion of full benefit	Effective tax rate
31 March 2020	100%	10%
31 March 2019	100%	10%
31 March 2018	100%	10%
31 March 2017	90%	11%
31 March 2016	80%	12%
31 March 2015	70%	13.3%
31 March 2014	60%	15.2%

10.3 Rights that can qualify

Although called the "Patent Box", other rights than patents can qualify, including:

- certain rights relating to the marketing of human and veterinary medicine;
- plant breeders' rights; and
- plant variety rights.

For the types of patents that can qualify see **10.4.2** below.

Reference is made in this book primarily to patents but the rules also apply to the other qualifying rights.

Law: CTA 2010, s. 357BB

10.4 Conditions to be met

10.4.1 Overview

To qualify for the Patent Box the owner of the IP must be a qualifying company. Such a company must meet the following three conditions in each accounting period in which the Patent Box applies:

- **Ownership condition** (Condition 1) – the qualifying company must hold a patent (or other qualifying right) or exclusive licence which has been granted within the EU (although patents granted by certain EU countries, such as France, do not qualify);
- **Development condition** (Condition 2) – the company or a company within the same group must have played a significant part in the development of the patent or of a product incorporating the patent; and
- **Active ownership condition** (Condition 3) – this condition only applies where the company is part of a group of companies. If it applies, the qualifying company must either have met the development condition itself or, where another group company has met the development condition, it must perform a significant amount of management activity in respect of the rights.

These conditions are considered in detail below.

To qualify for the relief an election must be made in the corporation tax return, specifying the first period for which it has effect. There is no specified form in which the claim should be made and so it should be included in the computation submitted with the corporation tax return (CT600). This election should be made by filing a tax return (or amending a filed return) within two years of the end of the accounting period. The election generally has effect for all subsequent periods but can be revoked.

Law: CTA 2010, s. 357A-357BE, 357G-357GA

10.4.2 Ownership

To satisfy the ownership condition a company must own or have an exclusive licence over a qualifying right. The list of rights which qualify are set by the legislation and include:

- a patent granted in the UK under the *Patent Act* 1977;
- a patent granted under the European Patent Convention;
- a similar right granted by another EEA state which is specified by the government. This list currently includes Austria, Bulgaria, the Czech Republic, Denmark, Estonia,

Finland, Germany, Hungary, Poland, Portugal, Romania, Slovakia and Sweden.

The patent must be valid to qualify for the relief (although relief is available for patents which are "pending" (see below)).

A company can be a qualifying company if it does not own the patent outright but has an exclusive licence to use it. An exclusive licence is one under which (CTA 2010, s. 357BA):

- the right is conferred to the exclusion of all other persons in one or more national territories; and:
- the holder of the licence either:
  - has the right to bring proceedings for infringement without the consent of the owner; or
  - is entitled to the majority of damages for infringement of the right.

It is possible to have more than one exclusive licence in a national territory providing that the field of use of the patent is sufficiently different. There are specific anti-avoidance rules relating to exclusive licences at CTA 2010, s. 357F.

Where a company does not directly own IP but is party to a "cost sharing arrangement" ("CSA") the ownership of other parties to the CSA can be used to meet the ownership condition. The detailed rules are found in CTA 2010, s. 357GC. Care should be taken when looking at the CSA rules as they were rewritten for accounting periods beginning on or after 1 April 2017. Further comment on the CSA rules is found in section **14.10**.

Law: CTA 2010, s. 357BA-357BB, 357GC

10.4.3 Development

Patent Box benefits are not aimed at companies that only have a passive interest in IP. There must be involvement in the innovation behind a patented invention or the application of that patented invention. The company (or another group company) must have undertaken qualifying development by:

- creating the invention;
- significantly contributing to the creation of the invention; or
- performing significant activity (in terms of costs, time or effort) to develop:
    - the patented invention;
    - any product incorporating the patented invention; or
    - any process incorporating the patented invention.

As mentioned above, the test can be met in various ways by companies within a group by satisfying one of a range of conditions (summarised below).

Condition A

This applies where the company undertook the qualifying development and has not ceased to be or become a controlled member of a group since that time.

Condition B

This applies where a company undertook the qualifying development itself but has since ceased to be or become a controlled member of a group.

To meet the development condition in these circumstances the company must continue to perform activities of the same description as the qualifying development for 12 months after joining or leaving the group. The company must remain a member of the new group, or must not become a member of another group (depending on the circumstances).

Condition C

This applies where a company is a member of a group but the qualifying development was undertaken by another company within the group ("B"). To meet the development condition in these circumstances the other company ("B") must have been a member of the group at the time it undertook the qualifying development. Note that the claimant did not need to be a member of the group at the time of the qualifying development.

Condition D

This applies where the company is a member of a group and another company ("B") which is, or has been, part of the group has carried on qualifying development. To meet the development condition one of the following conditions should also be met:

- B continues activities of the same description as the qualifying development for 12 months after joining the group; or
- B's trade is transferred to another member of the group ("C") and the transferor and transferee have together carried on activities of the same description as the qualifying development activity for 12 months. As such, the activity of B and C can be aggregated when deciding if this continued for 12 months.

Law: CTA 2010, s. 357BC-357BD
Guidance: CIRD 210190

10.4.4 Meaning of "group" for Patent Box purposes

A "group" for Patent Box purposes is defined widely, so careful consideration is required. A company ("A") is in a group with another company ("B") where for the relevant period or at the relevant time:

- the financial results of A and B are consolidated;
- A and B are connected (broadly where one company can control another or both are controlled by the same person);
- A has a major interest in B (or vice versa). A major interest is broadly where two entities have control of another entity with each party having an interest of 40% or more (a joint venture type arrangement);
- the financial results of A are consolidated with a third company and the third company has a major interest in B; or
- A and a third company are connected and the third company has a major interest in B.

Law: CTA 2010, s. 357GD

10.4.5 Active ownership condition

The *passive* holding of IP which the company did not develop itself should not qualify for the relief. Where the claimant company is within a group (see the preceding section) it will need to consider the active ownership condition. The company must:

- have undertaken the qualifying development work itself in relation to those rights; or
- have undertaken, during the accounting period, a *significant amount* of management activity in relation to those rights.

This means that if the company did not develop the intellectual property itself it must consider the active management condition in each accounting period.

HMRC have provided some guidance on what can be treated as management activity:

> "Activities such as deciding on whether to maintain protection in particular jurisdictions, grant licences, research alternative applications for the innovation or licensing others to do so, count as management activity.
>
> Similarly, where the rights are being exploited by incorporating the item into products, activities such as deciding on which products will go to market, what features those products will have and how and where they will be sold will also count as management activity."

The HMRC guidance suggests that the following factors are important in determining whether the management activity can be treated as significant:

"• The resources the company employs,
- The breadth of its responsibilities for the IP,
- The nature of the IP rights held and the amount of management they require, and

- The significance and impact of the decisions and plans it, as opposed to other group companies, makes in relation to that IP."

Law: CTA 2010, s. 357BE
Guidance: CIRD 210210

10.5 Making the most of Patent Box

To maximise the potential benefit from the relief, a full review should be undertaken to include:

- a review of the existing intellectual property (IP) portfolio;
- a review of whether any unprotected intellectual property should be protected to bring it within the Patent Box;
- an analysis of how the qualifying conditions are met for each item of intellectual property, and whether any adjustments should be made to ensure qualification;
- preparation of documentation illustrating how the qualifying criteria are met;
- a review of the accounting systems to ensure that it is possible to collect the appropriate sales information;
- consideration of streaming under the new scheme even if it does not yet apply;
- a review of whether the inputs to the R&D fraction can be tracked; and
- an analysis of the different elections.

11. How to approach the Patent Box

11.1 Introduction

For accounting periods beginning on or before 30 June 2016, the "new rules" do not apply and the company will make a claim under the "old rules". These "old rules" are covered in **Chapter 12**. The considerations set out below apply to the new rules – periods beginning on or after 1 July 2016.

The revisions to the Patent Box made in FA 2016 have increased the complications of the relief considerably. This should not be a reason not to make a claim, however, as the benefits for IP-rich businesses can still be significant. The legislation can appear to be tortuous at first glance but a route through the maze can be found as long as you are clear which path to go down from the start. For accounting periods beginning on or after 1 July 2021, all claims will need to apply the R&D fraction rules. Before 2021 the route you will take will depend on certain factors:

- whether the company is a new entrant or an old entrant – see section **11.3**;
- (if the claimant is an old entrant) whether the company has income from new IP or not – see section **11.4** below.

11.2 Preparing for the new regime

It is essential for all companies to have an understanding of the basics of the new regime even where it does not need to be applied straightaway; this will allow the company to be prepared for when it will apply. All claims from 2021 will need to apply the R&D fraction and so any company still making a claim then will need to have records in place to support the R&D fraction. These records should cover periods from 1 July 2016 or potentially before. This section includes a summary of the considerations, but more detailed guidelines are included at **14.4.2**.

The new rules require all claims to be streamed (so calculating patent-related profits by allocating expenses to the patent-related income) and not apportioned based on turnover. This streaming should ideally be done according to the individual IP rights. If this is not possible it may be acceptable to stream according to product, process or potentially the product family. A company should consider how it will stream its IP-related income (for example by rights or products) and start to track and trace its expenditure as soon as possible.

The new rules require the application of the R&D fraction, which reduces the benefit of the claim where expenditure is incurred on subcontracting certain R&D to connected parties or on the acquisition of the IP. This requires that the following are tracked for each sub-stream:

- in-house R&D expenditure;
- R&D expenditure subcontracted to a connected party;
- R&D expenditure subcontracted to an unconnected party;
- acquisition costs (potentially including licence fees).

Further details on the R&D fraction are included at section **14.8** and details on streaming and documentation are at **14.4.2**.

11.3 "New entrant" or "old entrant"

A company is treated as a new entrant where:

- the first period for which the company's Patent Box election (or most recent election) has effect *begins* on or after 1 July 2016; or
- the company elects to be treated as a new entrant.

The term "old entrant" is not defined in the legislation but covers all companies which are not a new entrant, so:

- the most recent Patent Box election was made for a period beginning before 1 July 2016; and
- no election has been made to be treated as a new entrant.

Where IP is transferred as part of the transfer of a trade it may be possible to look at the ownership of the transferor when considering whether the company is a new entrant (CTA 2010, s. 357GCA).

Law: CTA 2010, s. 357A(11), 357GCA

Guidance: CIRD 240160, 270100

11.4 Meaning of "new IP"

Broadly speaking, new IP is treated in the same way as IP owned by a new entrant. An IP right is treated as new if it meets either of the following conditions. All other IP rights, owned by an old entrant, are treated as old IP rights.

- **New patent** - where the patent was granted in response to an application which had been filed on or after 1 July 2016.
- **Grant or assignment of an exclusive licence or assignment of a patent** - where an exclusive licence is granted or assigned, or a patent is assigned, the IP is treated as new IP if the grant or assignment took place on or after 1 July 2016 (or on or after 2 January 2016 in certain circumstances where IP was transferred between connected parties).

Where the company is subject to a cost sharing arrangement (see section **14.10**), the ownership of the other party to the cost sharing arrangement should be considered when deciding if IP is new IP or old IP.

Law: CTA 2010, s. 357BP

Guidance: CIRD 270200

11.5 Navigating the Patent Box

As set out above, for accounting periods beginning on or before 30 June 2016, the pre-FA 2016 rules apply and these are covered in **Chapter 12**.

The different calculations are divided into different Chapters in the legislation. Until 2021 this applies as follows:

- Company is an old entrant with no new IP - this is dealt with in **Chapter 13** below.
- Company is a new entrant - this is dealt with in **Chapter 14**.
- Company is an old entrant with new IP - this is dealt with in **Chapter 15**.

For periods beginning on or after 1 July 2021, all claims will be treated in the same way as a new entrant.

The diagram below summarises how to navigate through the following chapters (assuming that no election is made to be treated as a new entrant):

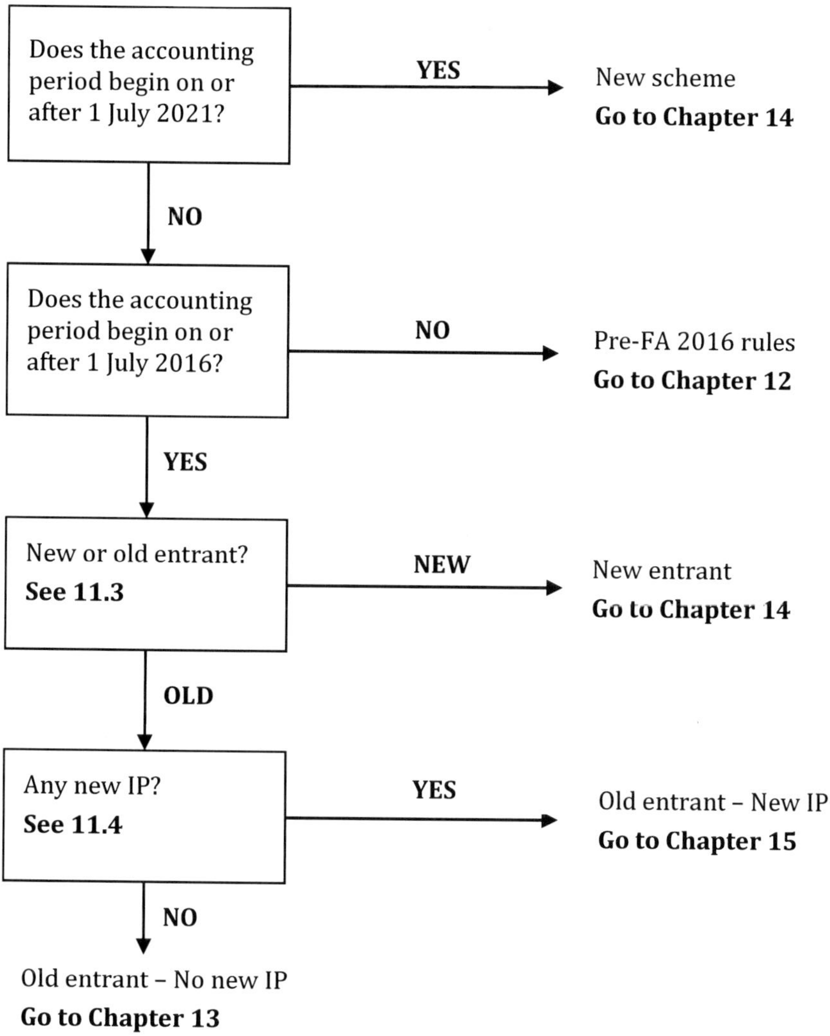

12. The pre-FA 2016 rules

12.1 Introduction

For accounting periods beginning on or before 30 June 2016 the company does not need to apply the new rules enacted in FA 2016. This chapter covers the calculation of the relevant profit for these periods.

Care should be taken when looking at the legislation as references included in this chapter refer to the legislation prior to FA 2016.

12.2 Calculating relevant IP profits

In summary, the calculation of the patent-derived profits has the following stages:

1. calculate the total gross income from the trade;
2. calculate the percentage of total income which is made up of patent-related income;
3. calculate the percentage of the profits of the trade which are patent related;
4. deduct the routine return (see below): the amount given by this step is the "qualifying residual profit";
5. (if claimed) deduct the small claims amount for the marketing royalty, and go to stage 7;
6. deduct the marketing asset (if not dealt with above in point 5);
7. (if elected for profits before grant) add the profits relating to periods before the grant of the patent.

It is possible to stream the profits rather than use the methodology set out above and in certain cases this is mandatory (see section **12.3**).

Law: CTA 2010, s. 357C, 357D

Step 1 – calculate the gross income of the trade

The gross income of the trade is the total of the following, when brought into account as a credit in calculating the profits of the trade for the period:

- revenue – recognised as such under GAAP, or would be were the accounts prepared under GAAP;
- compensation – damages, proceeds of insurance or compensation;
- adjustments on the change in the basis of assessment brought into account as receipts (under CTA 2009, s. 181);
- proceeds from intangible fixed assets (CTA 2009, Pt. 8, Ch. 4);
- profits from the sale of patent rights (CTA 2009, s. 912).

Gross income specifically excludes "finance income". Finance income is defined (CTA 2010, s. 357CB) as:

- credits treated as receipts of the trade in respect of loan relationships and derivatives;
- any amount arising from a financial asset in accordance with GAAP; and
- returns which are produced by an arrangement that is economically equivalent to interest (see CTA 2009, s. 486B for more detail on this).

Law: CTA 2010, s. 357CA-357CB

Step 2 – calculate the patent-related income percentage

First the relevant IP income ("RIPI") must be calculated. This calculation is possibly the most favourable aspect of the relief as it stands, as it can include a very wide range of income. Importantly, the sale of assets which incorporate a patented item can also qualify as patent-related income.

RIPI includes the following in respect of the qualifying right:

- income from the sale of:
  - a patented product;
  - a product incorporating the patented product; or

  - items wholly or mainly designed to be incorporated in the above (this is aimed at bespoke spare parts);
- licence fees and royalties received under an agreement granting another person:
  - a right in respect of the qualifying patent;
  - other rights in respect of the qualifying patent or *process*;
  - (where an agreement grants a right under the above) rights granted for the same purpose;
- income from the sale or disposal of the right;
- payments in respect of infringement, or alleged infringement;
- damages and the proceeds of insurance or compensation.

In addition, the company may elect to include a "notional royalty" to recognise the use of the patent within the company's business in a way that does not create RIPI under the above headings. For example, this could be using a patented manufacturing machine in the manufacturing process of an unpatented product, or using a patented item to provide a service to a customer. The value of the notional royalty is calculated using transfer pricing principles in line with the OECD *Model Tax Convention* and the OECD *Transfer Pricing Guidelines*.

Once the patent-related income has been calculated, it is then necessary to calculate the proportion this makes up of the total income, using the following formula:

(RIPI / TI) x 100

where:

RIPI = patent-related income

TI = total income

Ring fenced income related to oil extraction or oil rights, and certain income which is attributable to non-exclusive licences, are specifically excluded from being RIPI (CTA 2010, s. 357CE).

Under CTA 2010, s. 357CF a just and reasonable apportionment may be required where income relates either to:

- mixed income, where:
  - the proceeds of the sale of an item relate partly to the sale of a qualifying item and partly not, and
  - the items are sold together as a single unit (or part of one) for a single price; or
- a mixed agreement: where part of the income relating to an agreement relates to a qualifying IP right or exclusive licence and part does not, or if other services are included.

Law: CTA 2010, s. 357CC-357CF

Step 3 – calculate the percentage of the patent-related profits of the trade

First, calculate the profit of the trade with (broadly) the following adjustments:

- add:
  - debits in respect of loan relationships (CTA 2009, s. 297);
  - debits in respect of derivative contracts (CTA 2009, s. 573); and
  - the additional deduction relating to R&D tax relief (CTA 2009, Pt. 13), television production relief (Pt. 15A), video games development relief (Pt. 15B), and theatrical production relief (Pt. 15C).
- subtract:
  - the amount of the RDEC brought into account in calculating the profit of the trade; and
  - profits in respect of finance income (CTA 2010, s. 357CB).

An additional adjustment may be made to profits in respect of the following if there is a shortfall of expenditure in the year of claim:

- R&D expenditure (CTA 2010, s. 357CH);
- Qualifying expenditure on television production relief (CTA 2009, Pt. 15A) and video games development relief (CTA 2009, Pt. 15B) (CTA 2010, s. 357CHA).

The profits of the trade must then be allocated between profits relating to the patents and profits which do not relate to patents.

Law: CTA 2010, s. 357CG-357CHA

Step 4 – calculate the routine return

This aims to remove those profits which a business would have made in the absence of the intellectual property. The "routine return" is deemed to amount to 10% of specified deductions, as follows:

- capital allowances;
- costs of premises;
- personnel costs;
- plant and machinery costs;
- professional services; and
- various miscellaneous services.

This is apportioned between patent and non-patent profits and the relevant proportion is then deducted from the patent-related profits in the Patent Box profits calculation.

Law: CTA 2010, s. 357CI-357CK
Guidance: CIRD 220430-220460

Steps 5 and 6 – deduct the marketing asset return

After deducting the routine return from the patent-related profits a further deduction is made for returns from marketing assets. The marketing asset return is the excess of the "notional marketing royalty" in respect of the trade over the "actual marketing royalty" for that trade. This attempts to prevent returns from marketing assets from benefiting from the reduced tax rate. The legislation provides that the notional marketing royalty should be calculated under transfer pricing principles in line with the OECD *Model Tax Convention* and the OECD *Transfer Pricing Guidelines*. CTA 2010, s. 357CO sets out the rules for calculating the notional marketing royalty in detail.

For these purposes the relevant marketing assets of a company are:

- anything in respect of which passing off proceedings could be brought, including a registered trademark;
- signs or indications of geographical origin; and
- information relating to customers or potential customers of the company or a group company which is intended for use for marketing purposes.

If the notional marketing royalty, after deducting any actual royalty paid, would be less than 10% of the profits after deduction of the routine return then the notional marketing royalty is treated as being nil.

An election can be made for "small claims", which avoids the need to undertake a transfer pricing study. The detailed rules relating to the small claims election are included in CTA 2010, s. 357CL-357CM.

Law: CTA 2010, s. 357CL-357CP

Step 7 – (if elected for profits before grant) add the profits relating to periods before the grant of the patent

Where a company makes patent-related profits before the grant of the patent it can elect into the regime to receive benefit from the Patent Box.

To prevent companies from gaining the benefit for products which are not patentable, the benefit of the Patent Box is not received until the patent is granted. When the patent is granted the accumulated patent-related profits for the patent pending period are then included in the calculation for the period of grant. This extension applies to profits in an accounting period where:

- an election for Patent Box relief is in place;
- the company was a qualifying company in that period; and
- the period ends on or after the later of:
  - the first day of the period of six years ending on the grant of the qualifying right, or
  - the date of the filing of the patent application or grant of the exclusive licence.

Law: CTA 2010, s. 357CQ

12.3 Alternative streaming methodology for calculating patent-related profits

As an alternative to the proportional allocation of profits shown above, the company could elect to stream the profits of the trade between patent-related income and non-patent-related income. The profits of the different income streams should be calculated.

The method for calculating the RIPI where the streaming approach is used is set out in CTA 2010, s. 357DA.

Where certain conditions are met it is mandatory to stream the profits:

- if the trading profits include "substantial" amounts that are not fully recognised as income in accordance with GAAP;
- if the gross income includes substantial amounts of licensing income which is not RIPI; or
- if the company has income which is not RIPI, and it receives income from licences where the income relates to rights over which the company owns an exclusive licence.

"Substantial" is here defined as the lower of:

- £2 million; or
- 20% of the total gross income of the trade for the accounting period.

There is a *de minimis* limit whereby an amount is not treated as substantial if it does not exceed £50,000.

Law: CTA 2010, s. 357D-357DC

12.4 Relevant IP losses

It is possible to have relevant IP losses for a given period, which creates a set-off amount which is offset against RIPI of the company or other members of the group. CTA 2010, Pt. 8A, Ch. 5 covers the calculation and offset of these losses in detail.

The possibility that the company could have relevant IP losses should be considered when deciding whether to elect into the Patent Box regime, as if no election is in effect for a period the losses do not arise.

Law: CTA 2010, s. 357E-357EF

13. Old entrant – no new IP

13.1 Introduction

Where a company can still claim under the "old scheme" – and it does not have any new IP – the R&D fraction rules do not need to be applied. The rules below apply where no election has been made for the claimant to be treated as a new entrant.

Where a company could continue making claims for accounting periods beginning from 1 July 2021 then it should consider the new Patent Box rules now. In particular, the company should consider how it will stream its income and what records it will need to support this (see section **14.4.2**).

The legislation relating to old entrants with no new IP is found in CTA 2010, Pt. 8, Chapters 3 and 4.

13.2 Calculating relevant IP profits

In summary, the calculation of the patent-derived profits has the following stages:

1. calculate the total gross income from the trade;
2. calculate the percentage of total income which is made up of patent-related income;
3. calculate the percentage of the profits of the trade which are patent related;
4. deduct the routine return in relation to the trade for the accounting period (see below) – the amount given by this step is the "qualifying residual profit";
5. (if claimed) deduct the small claims amount for the marketing royalty, and go to stage 7;
6. deduct the marketing asset return in relation to the trade for the accounting period (if not dealt with above in point 5);
7. (if elected for profits before grant) add the profits relating to periods before the grant of the patent.

It is possible to stream the profits rather than use the methodology set out above and in certain cases this is mandatory (see section **13.3** below).

Law: CTA 2010, s. 357C, 357D

Step 1 – calculate the gross income of the trade

The gross income of the trade is calculated in the same way here as described for Step 1 at **12.2** above.

As before, gross income specifically excludes "finance income". Finance income is defined (this time by virtue of CTA 2010, s. 357BG) in the same way here as at **12.2**.

Law: CTA 2010, s. 357CA, 357BG

Step 2 – calculate the patent-related income percentage

First the relevant IP income ("RIPI") must be calculated. This calculation is made in the same way as is described at Step 2 at **12.2** above.

In addition, the company may elect to include a "notional royalty" to recognise the use of the patent within the company's business in a way that does not create RIPI under the above headings. Once more, see **12.2** for details.

Once the patent-related income has been calculated, it is then necessary to calculate the proportion this makes up of the total income using the following formula:

(RIPI / TI) x 100

where:

RIPI = patent-related income

TI = total income

Ring fenced income related to oil extraction or oil rights, and certain income which is attributable to non-exclusive licences, are specifically excluded from being RIPI (CTA 2010, s. 357BHB).

Under CTA 2010, s. 357BHC a just and reasonable apportionment may be required where income relates either to:

- mixed income:
  - where the proceeds of the sale of an item relate partly to the sale of a qualifying item and partly not, and
  - the items are sold together as a single unit (or part of one) for a single price; or
- a mixed agreement: where part of the income relating to an agreement relates to a qualifying IP right or exclusive licence and part does not, or if other services are included.

Law: CTA 2010, s. 357BH-357BHC

Step 3 – calculate the percentage of the patent-related profits of the trade

First, calculate the profit of the trade with (broadly) the following adjustments:

- add:
  - debits in respect of loan relationships (CTA 2009, s. 297);
  - debits in respect of derivative contracts (CTA 2009, s. 573); and
  - the additional deduction relating to R&D tax relief (CTA 2009, Pt. 13), television production relief (Pt. 15A), video games development relief (Pt. 15B), and theatrical production relief (Pt. 15C).
- subtract:
  - the amount of the RDEC brought into account in calculating the profit of the trade; and
  - profits in respect of finance income (CTA 2010, s. 357BG).

An additional adjustment may be made to profits in respect of the following if there is a shortfall of expenditure in the year of claim:

- R&D expenditure (CTA 2010, s. 357CH);
- Qualifying expenditure on television production relief (CTA 2009, Pt. 15A) and video games development relief (CTA 2009, Pt. 15B) (CTA 2010, s. 357CHA).

The profits of the trade must then be allocated between profits relating to the patents and profits which do not relate to patents.

Law: CTA 2010, s. 357CG-357CHA

Step 4 – calculate the routine return

This aims to remove those profits which a business would have made in the absence of the intellectual property. Once more, the rules here are exactly the same as outlined at Step 4 at **12.2** above (though the statutory path is different).

Law: CTA 2010, s. 357CI, 357BJA, 357BJB
Guidance: CIRD 220430-220460

Steps 5 and 6 – deduct the marketing asset return

After deducting the routine return from the patent-related profits a further deduction is made for returns from marketing assets. Again, the rules are identical to those described for the equivalent Steps at **12.2** above.

Law: CTA 2010, s. 357CL-357CP

Step 7 – (if elected for profits before grant) add the profits relating to periods before the grant of the patent

Where a company makes patent-related profits before the grant of the patent it can elect into the regime to receive benefit from the Patent Box. Once more, the rules are identical to those described for Step 7 at **12.2** above.

Law: CTA 2010, s. 357CQ

13.3 Alternative streaming methodology for calculating patent-related profits

As an alternative to the proportional allocation of profits shown above, the company could elect to stream the profits of the trade between patent-related income and non-patent-related income. The profits of the different income streams should be calculated.

The rules here are identical to those described at **12.3** above.

Law: CTA 2010, s. 357D-357DC

13.4 Relevant IP losses

It is possible to have relevant IP losses for a given period, which creates a set-off amount which is offset against RIPI of the company or other members of the group. CTA 2010, Pt. 8A, Ch. 5 covers the calculation and offset of these losses in detail.

The possibility that the company could have relevant IP losses should be considered when deciding whether to elect into the Patent Box regime, as if no election is in effect for a period the losses do not arise.

Law: CTA 2010, s. 357E-357EF

14. New entrant

14.1 Introduction

Finance Act 2016 not only added complexity to the Patent Box through the introduction of the R&D fraction (amongst other aspects) but also added to the documentation requirements. This chapter deals with the calculation under the new regime, including the complexities of the R&D fraction and the F(No. 2)A 2017 "cost sharing arrangement" rules.

14.2 Calculating relevant IP profits – summary

Under the new regime the patent-related profits must be calculated using streaming. In summary, the calculation of the patent-derived profits has the following stages:

1. Take the credits brought into account in calculating the profits of the trade for the accounting period (other than finance income) and divide them into two streams:
    a. relevant IP income "RIPI"; and
    b. the "standard income stream" – amounts that are not relevant IP income.
2. Divide the RIPI into sub-streams according to whether the income is attributable to a particular:
    a. IP right – the "individual IP right sub-stream";
    b. kind of IP item – the "product sub-stream";
    c. kind of IP process – the "process sub-stream".
3. Allocate the debits relating to the standard income stream and the various sub-streams.
4. Deduct from each sub-stream:
    a. the amount allocated under Step 3; and
    b. the routine return for the sub-stream (see below);
5. (Where the amount after Step 4 is more than nil) deduct the marketing asset return for each sub-stream.
6. Apply the "R&D fraction" to each sub-stream.
7. Add the sub-stream amounts together.

8. (If elected for profits before grant) add the profits relating to periods before the grant of the patent.

Law: CTA 2010, s. 357BF
Guidance: CIRD 275000

14.3 Step 1 – divide credits into relevant IP income stream and standard income stream

The amounts which are brought into account in calculating the profits of a trade for the accounting period, apart from finance income, should be divided into two streams:

- the relevant IP income stream; and
- the standard income stream.

RIPI includes the following in respect of the qualifying right:

- income from the sale of:
    - a patented product;
    - a product incorporating the patented product; or
    - items wholly or mainly designed to be incorporated in the above (this is aimed at bespoke spare parts);
- licence fees and royalties received under an agreement granting another person:
    - a right in respect of the qualifying patent;
    - other rights in respect of the qualifying patent or *process*;
    - (where an agreement grants a right under the above) rights granted for the same purpose;
- income from the sale or disposal of the right;
- payments in respect of infringement, or alleged infringement;
- damages and the proceeds of insurance or compensation.

In addition the company may elect to include a "notional royalty" to recognise the use of the patent within the company's business in a way which does not create RIPI under the above heads. For example, this could be using a patented manufacturing machine in the manufacturing process of an unpatented product or using a patented item to provide a service to a customer. The value of the notional royalty is calculated using transfer pricing principles in line with the OECD *Model Tax Convention* and the OECD *Transfer Pricing Guidelines*. For companies qualifying for small claims treatment a simplified method of calculation can be used (CTA 2010, s. 357BNA).

Finance income is defined in CTA 2010, s. 357BG as:

- credits treated as receipts of the trade in respect of loan relationships and derivatives;
- any amount arising from a financial asset in accordance with generally accepted accounting practice; and
- returns which are produced by an arrangement that is economically equivalent to interest (see CTA 2009, s. 486B for more detail on this).

Ring fenced income related to oil extraction or oil rights, and certain income which is attributable to non-exclusive licences, are specifically excluded from being RIPI (CTA 2010, s. 357BHB).

Under CTA 2010, s. 357BHC a just and reasonable apportionment may be required where income relates either to:

- mixed income:
  - where the proceeds of the sale of an item relate partly to the sale of a qualifying item and part not, and
  - the items are sold together as a single unit (or part of one) for a single price; or
- a mixed agreement: where part of the income relating to an agreement relates to a qualifying IP right or exclusive licence and part does not or if other services are included.

Law: CTA 2010, s. 357BH-357BHC, 357BNA
Guidance: CIRD 275000

14.4 Step 2 – divide the RIPI stream income into sub-streams

14.4.1 Introduction

Divide the RIPI into sub-streams according to whether the income is attributable to a particular:

1. IP right – the "individual IP right sub-stream" (or product family);
2. kind of IP item – the "product sub-stream";
3. kind of IP process – the "process sub-stream".

Where possible the income should be streamed according to each particular IP right ((1) above). You should only apply an approach including the product or process sub-streams ((2) and (3) above) where it is not reasonably practicable to use the individual IP right sub-stream approach. When applying (2) and (3), items and processes are treated as being of a particular kind when they are intended to be, or are capable of being, used for substantially the same purpose or purposes.

To reduce the administrative burden of the sub-stream approach, new entrants are able to make an election to aggregate the sub-streams (the "global streaming election" (CTA 2010, s. 357BNC)). This is available for companies which meet the criteria to be treated as a small claim. The effect of the election is, broadly, to omit Step 2 from the calculation so that there are generally only two streams.

Law: CTA 2010, s. 357BF(2)
Guidance: CIRD 273200

14.4.2 How to decide the level of streaming

It is possible to stream according to IP right, product or process. The starting point when deciding on the level of streaming is to track at the level of the IP right rather than the type of product or process, if possible. Where it is not reasonably practicable to use the individual IP right then streaming at product or process level should be acceptable. The key driver behind this is whether it is possible to track and trace the income and expenditure relating to the sub-stream. Section **14.4.3** covers tracking and tracing.

Where the product sub-stream approach is applied, and it is not possible to allocate income and expenditure between individual products, HMRC state that it is possible to stream at product family level. HMRC state that to do this the products should be intended to be used substantially for the same purpose. HMRC give the following guidance on the use of family level streaming:

> "A company cannot choose to place its entire relevant income within one product family, unless it is all of the same kind and is unable to otherwise separately identify income from the different IP assets. It should be noted that whilst this might be easier from an income perspective, there can be implications in applying the R&D fraction. For example, if one of the items should subsequently be developed so it includes an acquired qualifying IP right the R&D fraction will be reduced for all of that stream."

The legislation does not restrict the ability of the company to change its method from one year to another. HMRC's manuals state that: "such a change should be supported by an explanation of the underlying reason for making the change." If a change is made it is advisable that some description of the reasoning behind the change and supporting evidence is submitted at the same time as the claim.

Guidance: CIRD 271500

14.4.3 Tracking and tracing

In order to allocate income, and to calculate the R&D fraction for a sub-stream, a company must be able to track its income and expenditure to that particular sub-stream.

If a company is clear that it has an R&D fraction which gives a result of 1, the company does not have to carry out tracking and tracing for each sub-stream. In their guidance HMRC state that:

> "If a company has clear evidence that all of their fractions cannot be other than 1 (for example because all the R&D has been carried out in-house and there have been no related acquisitions) and chooses, under self assessment, to use this evidence instead of tracking and tracing actual R&D expenditure, HMRC will consider this to be acceptable."

See below for further considerations of when to track and trace, for example future changes to the R&D fraction.

HMRC's guidance on the nature of the records states that the company should be able to explain the methodology used for allocating the expenditure in the first year and then should detail any significant changes to the method thereafter (CIRD 272100).

Guidance: CIRD 272000-273100

When to start tracking and tracing

For cases where streaming is not currently required, HMRC stress the importance of considering the future when deciding whether to begin to collect information to track and trace, for example if a company claims under the global streaming election but in later years exceeds the limits of qualification. At this stage the company will then require historic information to calculate the R&D fraction for each sub-stream. It is advisable to have a method for tracking and tracing in place even if not currently required.

Compulsory tracking and tracing can begin on a number of dates, depending on the facts, and is set by reference to the relevant period (see section **14.8.7**). The "relevant period" ends on the last day of the accounting period.

Where there is insufficient information to track and trace prior to 1 July 2016, it is possible to elect to use 1 July 2016 as the date on which tracking and tracing commences. The detailed rules for the election are included in CTA 2010, s. 357BLG and are covered at **14.8.7**.

Law: CTA 2010, s. 357BLF, 357BLG

When to stop tracking and tracing

Where a patent is out of protection the expenditure relating to it is no longer included in the R&D fraction and tracking of the expenditure will no longer be required.

14.5 Step 3 – allocate debits to sub-streams

Now that the RIPI of each sub-stream has been calculated the next step is to apportion the debits which are brought into account in calculating the profits of the trade for the accounting period. The debits should be allocated to the standard income stream and the various sub-streams. The debits should be allocated on a just and reasonable basis.

Certain "excluded debits" are not allocated. CTA 2010, s. 357BI sets out the excluded debits, which are:

- debits in respect of loan relationships (CTA 2009, s. 297);
- debits in respect of derivative contracts (CTA 2009, s. 573); and
- the additional deduction relating to R&D tax relief (CTA 2009, Pt. 13), television production relief (Pt. 15A), video games development relief (Pt. 15B), and theatrical production relief (Pt. 15C).

14.6 Step 4 – deduct debits and routine return

The debits allocated under Step 3 are then deducted from the sub-streams along with a routine return.

Certain expenditure which is directly related to income received by the company in respect of a qualifying right is not deducted where it is treated as an "income-related payment". An example could be a licence payment which is directly related to the company's sales of a qualifying item. Further details on this are given at CTA 2010, s. 357BIA.

The routine return aims to remove those profits which a business would have made in the absence of the intellectual property. The routine return is deemed to amount to 10% of specified deductions, which are allocated to the sub-stream at Step 3, as follows:

- capital allowances;
- costs of premises;
- personnel costs;
- plant and machinery costs;
- professional services; and
- various miscellaneous services.

Law: CTA 2010, s. 357BJ-357BJB

14.7 Step 5 – deduct the marketing asset return

If the amount calculated under Step 4 for a sub-stream is more than nil then a marketing asset return should be deducted. The marketing asset return is the excess of the "notional marketing royalty" in respect of the sub-stream over the "actual marketing royalty" for that sub-stream. This attempts to prevent returns from marketing assets from benefiting from the reduced tax rate. The legislation provides that the notional marketing royalty should be calculated under transfer pricing principles in line with the OECD *Model Tax Convention* and the OECD *Transfer Pricing Guidelines*. CTA 2010, s. 357BKA sets out the rules for calculating the notional marketing royalty in detail.

For these purposes the relevant marketing assets of a company are:

- anything in respect of which passing off proceedings could be brought, including a registered trademark;
- signs or indications of geographical origin; and
- information relating to customers or potential customers of the company or a group company which is intended for use for marketing purposes.

If the notional marketing royalty, after deducting any actual royalty paid, would be less than 10% of the profits for the sub-stream after deduction of the routine return then the marketing royalty is treated as being nil.

An election can be made for "small claims" which avoids the need to undertake a transfer pricing study. The detailed rules relating to the small claims election are included in CTA 2010, s. 357BN-357BNB.

Law: CTA 2010, s. 357BK-357BKB, 357BN, 357BNB

14.8 Step 6 – the "R&D fraction"

14.8.1 Introduction

The R&D fraction must be applied separately to each sub-stream. The fraction is capped at 1 so that the RIPI cannot be increased. Although several of the definitions of the R&D tax reliefs are used there is no requirement to have made an R&D claim.

The R&D fraction is:

$$\frac{(D + S1) * 1.3}{D + S1 + S2 + A}$$

where:

D is the company's expenditure on relevant R&D undertaken in-house;

S1 is the company's qualifying expenditure on relevant R&D subcontracted to unconnected persons;

S2 is the company's qualifying expenditure on relevant R&D subcontracted to connected persons; and

A is the company's expenditure on acquisition of relevant IP rights.

The company must consider the expenditure which relates to the relevant period (see **14.8.7**). The R&D fraction should be reviewed annually to adjust for changes to the inputs.

Expenditure can relate to more than one stream, so an analysis of which sub-stream it relates to must be undertaken. HMRC guidance accepts that this might not be appropriate to allocate the expenditure between streams and an amount could be applied to more than one stream (CIRD 274200).

For accounting periods beginning on or after 1 April 2017, where a company is party to a cost sharing arrangement ("CSA"), the R&D fraction calculation can be affected by the following:

- R&D undertaken or contracted out by another party to the CSA (CTA 2010, s. 357GCZC);
- acquisition of qualifying IP rights by another party to the CSA (CTA 2010, s. 357GCZD);
- expenditure in connection with the formation of the CSA (CTA 2010, s. 357GCZE); and
- income in connection with the formation of the CSA (CTA 2010, s. 357GCZF)

The methodology for the calculation where the above CSA rules are applied is included in CTA 2010, s. 357BLEA.

Law: CTA 2010, s. 357BL, 357BLA, 357BLEA, 357GCZC-GCZF
Guidance: CIRD 274200

14.8.2 Relevant research and development

The term "relevant research and development" is defined for D, S1 and S2 at CTA 2010, s. 357BLB (5) and (6).

R&D is defined, as with the R&D relief, at CTA 2009, s. 1138. The definition of relevant research and development necessarily depends on what level of streaming the company is applying.

Individual IP right sub-stream – To be relevant R&D for the individual IP right sub-stream the R&D must relate to the qualifying IP to which the income included in the sub-stream is attributable.

Product sub-stream – To be relevant R&D for the product sub-stream the R&D must relate to the qualifying IP right granted in respect of any item to which the income in the sub-stream is attributable or which is incorporated in an item to which the income in the sub-stream is attributable.

Process sub-stream – To be relevant R&D for the process sub-stream the R&D must relate to the qualifying IP right granted in respect of any process to which the income in the sub-stream is attributable or which is incorporated in a process to which the income in the sub-stream is attributable.

R&D work "relates" to an IP right where the work:

- contributes to the creation of the invention;
- is undertaken for the purpose of developing the invention or ways the invention may be used or applied; or
- is undertaken for the purpose of developing an item or process incorporating the invention.

14.8.3 Qualifying expenditure on relevant R&D undertaken in-house

There is some reassurance in the fact that the definitions from the R&D tax relief are used and so are familiar to users of that regime. Care should be taken, however, as the application is not exactly the same. For example, payment of the R&D expenditure is not required for the Patent Box but is required for certain costs to qualify for the R&D relief.

This expenditure must be incurred by the company in the relevant period (see section **14.8.7**) and must meet both of the following conditions:

Condition A – the expenditure is incurred on the following:

- staffing costs (CTA 2009, s. 1123 and 1124) (see **5.4.3**);
- software (CTA 2009, s. 1125 to 1126B) (see **5.4.4**);
- consumable items or transformable stores, for example water, heat and power (CTA 2009, s. 1125 to 1126B) (see **5.4.4**);
- externally provided workers – broadly these are staff provided by other parties, such as employment agencies or other group companies (CTA 2009, s. 1127 to 1132) (see **5.4.5**);
- relevant payments made as part of clinical trials (CTA 2009, s. 1140) (see **5.4.6**).

Condition B – the expenditure is attributable to relevant R&D undertaken by the company itself.

Expenditure is treated as incurred in the relevant period only if the expenditure is allowable as a deduction for the trade for an accounting period which falls, in whole or in part, within the relevant period (CTA 2010, s. 357BLF(7)). See section **14.8.7** for the meaning of relevant period.

A company can claim an exemption for profits or losses of a foreign permanent establishment, the branch exemption (CTA 2009, s. 18A). Where the branch exemption applies for a period, an element of the branch's relevant R&D expenditure undertaken in-house is treated as expenditure on relevant R&D subcontracted to connected persons.

Law: CTA 2010, s. 37BLB

Guidance: CIRD 274300

14.8.4 Qualifying expenditure on relevant R&D subcontracted to unconnected persons

This is expenditure incurred by the company in the relevant period on a payment relating to relevant R&D to a subcontractor who is not connected to the company (see **5.4.2** for discussion on connection).

Where the payment relates in part to relevant R&D and in part to other matters the element properly attributable to other matters is disregarded for the calculation of the R&D fraction.

Expenditure is treated as incurred in the relevant period (see section **14.8.7**) only if the expenditure is allowable as a deduction for the trade for an accounting period which falls, in whole or in part, within the relevant period (CTA 2010, s. 357BLF(7)).

A company can claim an exemption for profits or losses of a foreign permanent establishment, the branch exemption (CTA 2009, s. 18A). Where the branch exemption applies for a period, an element of the branch's expenditure subcontracted to an unconnected party is treated as R&D expenditure subcontracted to connected persons.

Law: CTA 2010, s. 357BLC
Guidance: CIRD 274400

14.8.5 Qualifying expenditure on relevant R&D subcontracted to connected persons

This expenditure is the total of:

- expenditure incurred by the company in the relevant period on a payment relating to relevant R&D to a subcontractor who is connected to the company (see **5.4.2** for discussion on connection);
- expenditure treated as subcontracted to a connected person as a result of relating to foreign branches which are subject to the branch exemption (see **14.8.3** and **14.8.4**).

Where the payment relates in part to relevant R&D and in part to other matters the element properly attributable to other matters is disregarded.

Expenditure is treated as incurred in the relevant period (see section **14.8.7**) only if the expenditure is allowable as a deduction for the trade for an accounting period which falls, in whole or in part, within the relevant period (CTA 2010, s. 357BLF(7)).

Law: CTA 2010, s. 357BLD
Guidance: CIRD 274400

14.8.6 *Qualifying expenditure on acquisition of relevant qualifying IP rights*

Qualifying expenditure on acquisition of relevant qualifying IP rights is incurred by the company in the relevant period on a payment relating to any of the following:

- a payment made to a person in respect of the assignment by that person of a relevant qualifying IP right to the company;
- a payment made to a person for the grant or transfer by that person of an exclusive licence in respect of a relevant qualifying IP right; or
- a payment made to a person in respect of the disclosure by that person of any item or process where the company is granted a relevant qualifying IP right in respect of that item or process (or an item or process derived from it).

Where the company makes a series of payments in respect of the above then the payments are treated as made on the date of the first payment in the series.

HMRC guidance states that this category includes annual fees in respect of an exclusive licence, so ongoing licence payments will affect the R&D calculation.

Law: CTA 2010, s. 357BLE
Guidance: CIRD 274500

Relevant qualifying IP rights

The qualifying IP right for the individual IP right sub-stream is the IP right to which the income in the sub-stream is attributable.

The qualifying IP right for the product sub-stream is the IP right granted in respect of an item to which the income in the sub-stream is attributable, or which is incorporated in an item to which the income in the sub-stream is attributable.

The qualifying IP right for the process sub-stream is the IP right granted in respect of a process to which the income in the sub-stream is attributable, or which is incorporated in a process to which the income in the sub-stream is attributable.

14.8.7 Relevant period

The period for which expenditure should be included in the R&D fraction is called the relevant period. Reference to relevant period for the calculation of the R&D fraction is defined by CTA 2010, s. 357BLF.

The following table sets out the commencement date of the relevant period (for periods ending before 1 July 2036). It is possible to elect for the period to commence on an earlier date.

Criteria	Relevant period commencement date
Company is a new entrant and the accounting period begins before 1 July 2021	1 July 2013 (subject to "insufficient information" proviso below)
All other cases	1 July 2016

For periods ending on or after 1 July 2036 the relevant period is the 20-year period ending with the end of the accounting period.

The relevant period ends on the last day of the accounting period.

Expenditure is treated as incurred in the relevant period only if the expenditure is allowable as a deduction for the trade for an accounting period which falls, in whole or in part, within the relevant period for the following:

- qualifying expenditure on relevant R&D undertaken in-house;
- qualifying expenditure on relevant R&D subcontracted to unconnected persons; and
- qualifying expenditure on relevant R&D subcontracted to connected persons.

Law: CTA 2010, s. 357BLF

Election for earlier date

It is possible to elect for an earlier date to be treated as the start of the relevant period. The day elected cannot be more than 20 years before the last day of the accounting period. This could be beneficial where, for example, there was R&D expenditure before the relevant date.

Insufficient information about pre-enactment expenditure

A new entrant with insufficient information to support the R&D fraction prior to 1 July 2016 can elect to use a later date as the start of its relevant period. These rules can apply for accounting periods beginning before 1 July 2021.

Where a successful election is made for periods beginning before 1 July 2019, the relevant period for the sub-stream is the three years to the end of the accounting period.

Where a successful election is made for a period beginning on or after 1 July 2019, the relevant period for the sub-stream in particular begins on 1 July 2016.

Law: CTA 2010, s. 357BLG

14.8.8 Election to increase the R&D fraction for exceptional circumstances

In circumstances where a company believes that exceptional circumstances have resulted in an R&D fraction for a sub-stream which does not reasonably represent the R&D undertaken in-house or by unconnected parties, it should consider making an election under CTA 2010, s. 357BLH.

The election can be made for a sub-stream where, but for the increase resulting from an election under CTA 2010, s. 357BLH, the R&D fraction would:

- not be less than 0.325; and
- due to exceptional circumstances, be lower than the "value fraction".

The value fraction represents a just and reasonable assessment of the proportion of the value of the relevant qualifying IP rights which is attributable to the R&D undertaken at any time:

- by the company; or
- on behalf of the company by persons not connected with the company.

If successfully claimed, the R&D fraction is increased by the difference between the R&D fraction and the value fraction.

An election must be made giving notice to HMRC by the deadline for amending the corporation tax return.

Law: CTA 2010, s. 357BLH

Guidance: CIRD 275500

14.9 Step 8 – (if elected for profits before grant) add the profits relating to periods before the grant of the patent.

Where a company makes patent-related profits before the grant of the patent it can elect into the regime to receive benefit from the Patent Box.

To prevent companies from gaining the benefit for products which are not patentable, the benefit of the Patent Box is not received until the patent is granted. When the patent is granted the accumulated patent-related profits for the patent pending period are then included in the calculation for the period of grant. This extension applies to profits in an accounting period where:

- an election for Patent Box relief is in place;
- the company was a qualifying company in that period; and
- the period ends on or after the later of:
  - the first day of the period of six years ending on the grant of the qualifying right, or
  - the date of the filing of the patent application or grant of the exclusive licence.

Where a company is not streaming at the qualifying IP right level, it may need to recalculate its R&D fractions to reflect the new IP.

Law: CTA 2010, s. 357BM

14.10 Cost sharing arrangement ("CSA")

14.10.1 Introduction

If the company is treated as being a party to a CSA where one of the other parties to the CSA owns qualifying IP then it can also be treated as owning the qualifying IP right.

There are three other facets to the new CSA rules; they can impact:

- the rules regarding new and old IP (see section **11.4**).
- the R&D fraction (see section **14.8**).
- RIPI, as certain income related to the formation of a CSA can be treated as RIPI.

The rules relating to CSAs were rewritten in *Finance (No. 2) Act* 2017. These rules apply for accounting periods beginning on or after 1 April 2017.

The *Explanatory Notes* to F(No. 2)A 2017 state, in relation to the new CSA rules, that:

> "... the result is that the company's own contribution to the development work drives the amount of profit benefiting from the reduced rate."

For accounting periods beginning before 1 April 2017, the CSA rules related only to the ownership requirement. This has been broadly reproduced in the new CSA rules. The key difference between the original CSA definition and the F(No. 2)A 2017 definition is that the requirement that a party to the CSA holds a qualifying IP right or exclusive licence in respect of a qualifying IP right has been removed. The *Explanatory Notes* state that this change was made to recognise that a CSA may, at the outset, have no IP but may intend to develop it.

Law: CTA 2010, s. 357GC-357GCZF

14.10.2 What is a CSA?

The meaning of a CSA is set out in CTA 2010, s. 357GC, but (as noted above) care should be taken to ensure that the correct definition is used with the new rules applying for periods beginning on or after 1 April 2017. A CSA under the F(No. 2)A 2017 rules is an arrangement under which all of the following conditions are met:

1. Each party is required to contribute to the cost of, or undertake activities for the purpose of, creating or developing an item or process,
2. Each party:

  - is entitled to a share of the income attributable to the item or process, or
  - has one or more rights in respect of the item or process; and
3. The amount of any income received by each party is proportionate to its participation in the arrangement in terms of its contribution to the cost or activity (described in Condition 1).

As noted above, for periods beginning before 1 April 2017, there was an additional requirement that a party to the CSA had to hold a qualifying IP right or exclusive licence over such a right.

14.11 Application to transferred trades

Where trades are transferred in given circumstances, CTA 2010, s. 357GCA sets out rules that attribute expenditure incurred by the transferor to the transferee. In addition, in certain circumstances, expenditure incurred by the transferee in respect of the assignment, grant or transfer can be ignored for the calculation of the R&D fraction.

Law: CTA 2010, s. 357GCA
Guidance CIRD 240160, 271100

14.12 Relevant IP losses

It is possible to have relevant IP losses for a given period, which creates a set-off amount which is offset against RIPI of the company or other members of the group. CTA 2010, Pt. 8A, Ch. 5 covers the calculation and offset of these losses in detail.

The possibility that the company could have relevant IP losses should be considered when deciding whether to elect into the Patent Box regime, as if no election is in effect for a period the relevant IP losses do not arise.

Law: CTA 2010, s. 357E-357EF

15. Old entrant – new IP

15.1 Introduction

For periods beginning before 1 July 2021, a company which is an old entrant (see section **11.3**) but which has new IP (see section **11.4**) has to apply the R&D fraction only to its income relating to new IP. This is covered in Chapter 2B of Part 8A. The rules for new IP within the old scheme include specific rules relating to products or processes including both new IP and old IP (see **15.4.2** below).

15.2 Calculating relevant IP profits

In summary, the calculation of the patent-derived profits has the following stages:

1. Take the credits brought into account in calculating the profits of the trade for the accounting period (other than finance income) and divide them into two streams:
    a. relevant IP income "RIPI"; and
    b. the "standard income stream" – amounts that are not relevant IP income.
2. Divide the RIPI into sub-streams according to whether the income is attributable to :
    a. old qualifying IP rights – the "old IP rights sub-stream",
    b. new qualifying IP rights – the "individual IP right sub-stream";
    c. kind of IP item – the "product sub-stream";
    d. kind of IP process – the "process sub-stream".
3. Allocate the debits relating to the standard income stream and the various sub-streams.
4. Deduct from each sub-stream:
    a. the amount allocated under Step 3; and
    b. the routine return for the sub-stream (see below).
5. (Where the amount after Step 4 is more than nil) deduct the marketing asset return for each sub-stream.

6. Apply the "R&D fraction" to the individual IP right sub-stream, each product sub-stream and each process sub-stream (i.e. not the old IP rights sub-stream).
7. Add together:
    a. the amount of any old IP rights sub-stream from step 5, and
    b. the amount of each of the individual IP right sub-streams, each of the product sub-streams and each of the process sub-streams from Step 6.
8. (If elected for profits before grant) add the profits relating to periods before the grant of the patent.

Law: CTA 2010, s. 357BQ

15.3 Step 1 – divide credits into relevant IP income stream and standard income stream

The amounts which are brought into account in calculating the profits of a trade for the accounting period, apart from finance income, should be divided into two streams:

- the relevant IP income stream; and
- the standard income stream.

RIPI includes the following in respect of the qualifying right:

- income from the sale of:
    - a patented product;
    - a product incorporating the patented product; or
    - items wholly or mainly designed to be incorporated in the above (this is aimed at bespoke spare parts);
- licence fees and royalties received under an agreement granting another person:
    - a right in respect of the qualifying patent;
    - other rights in respect of the qualifying patent or *process*;
    - (where an agreement grants a right under the above) rights granted for the same purpose;
- income from the sale or disposal of the right;

- payments in respect of infringement, or alleged infringement;
- damages and the proceeds of insurance or compensation.

In addition the company may elect to include a "notional royalty" to recognise the use of the patent within the company's business in a way which does not create RIPI under the above heads. For example, this could be using a patented manufacturing machine in the manufacturing process of an unpatented product or using a patented item to provide a service to a customer. The value of the notional royalty is calculated using transfer pricing principles in line with the OECD *Model Tax Convention* and the OECD *Transfer Pricing Guidelines*. For companies qualifying for small claims treatment a simplified method of calculation can be used (CTA 2010, s. 357BNA).

Finance income is defined in CTA 2010, s. 357BG as:

- credits treated as receipts of the trade in respect of loan relationships and derivatives;
- any amount arising from a financial asset in accordance with generally accepted accounting practice; and
- returns which are produced by an arrangement that is economically equivalent to interest (see CTA 2009, s. 486B for more detail on this).

Ring fenced income related to oil extraction or oil rights, and certain income which is attributable to non-exclusive licences, are specifically excluded from being RIPI (CTA 2010, s. 357BHB).

Under CTA 2010, s. 357BHC a just and reasonable apportionment may be required where income relates either to:

- mixed income:
    - where the proceeds of the sale of an item relate partly to the sale of a qualifying item and part not, and
    - the items are sold together as a single unit (or part of one) for a single price; or

- a mixed agreement: where part of the income relating to an agreement relates to a qualifying IP right or exclusive licence and part does not, or if other services are included.

Law: CTA 2010, s. 357BH-357BHC, 357BNA
Guidance: CIRD 275000

15.4 Step 2 – divide the RIPI stream income into sub-streams

15.4.1 Introduction

Divide the RIPI into sub-streams according to whether the income is attributable to a particular:

1. old IP right – the "old individual IP right sub-stream" ;
2. new IP right – the "new individual IP right sub-stream";
3. kind of IP item – the "product sub-stream";
4. kind of IP process – the "process sub-stream".

Where possible the new IP right income should be streamed according to each particular IP right ((2) above). You should only apply an approach including the product or process sub-streams ((3) and (4) above) where it is not reasonably practicable to use the individual IP right sub-stream approach.

Where applying (3) and (4), items and processes are treated as being of a particular kind where they are intended to be or are capable of being used for substantially the same purpose or purposes.

New entrants are able to make an election to aggregate the sub-streams (the "global streaming election" (CTA 2010, s. 357BNC)). The global streaming election is not available to old entrants with new IP (claiming under Chapter 2B) and so to benefit from the election you have to accept that the R&D fraction rules will apply to all qualifying IP rights.

15.4.2 Mixed old and new income

Specific rules are included in the legislation covering how to treat cases where income which is allocated to either the product or process sub-stream (or product family) relates to both new and old IP.

All of the income can be treated for the purposes of Step 2 as relating to the old qualifying IP rights sub-stream where either:

- the value of the IP item or IP process relates wholly or mainly to old qualifying IP rights ("core value test"); or
- the old IP percentage is 80% or more ("numeric value test").

Where the old IP percentage is less than 80% but not less than 20% then the percentage is used to allocate the income to the old IP right sub-stream.

Where the percentage is less than 20% then no income is allocated to the old IP right sub-stream.

The company has the choice of whether to apply the core value or numeric value test. This should be reconsidered, and the numeric value test recalculated, where further IP right is incorporated into the product or process.

Test	**Condition**	**Proportion of income treated as related to old IP right sub-stream**
Core value	Value of the IP relates wholly or mainly to old qualifying IP rights	100%
Numeric value	old IP percentage 80% or more	100%
Numeric value	old IP percentage < 80% but ≥ 20%	20% to 80% depending on the old IP percentage
Numeric value	old IP percentage <20%	0%

HMRC provide their view on the application in detailed examples at CIRD 271600.

Law: CTA 2010, s. 357BQ

Calculating the old IP percentage

This is calculated as follows based on the number of items or processes.

$$\frac{O}{T} \times 100$$

where:

> **O** is the number of items or processes incorporated which relate to an old qualifying IP right; and
>
> **T** is the number of items or processes incorporated which relate to either an old qualifying IP right or a new qualifying IP right.

15.4.3 How to decide the level of streaming

It is possible to stream according to IP right, product or process. The starting point when deciding on the level of streaming is to track at the level of the IP right rather than the type of product or process, if possible. Where it is not reasonably practicable to apply an approach using the individual IP right, then streaming at product or process level should be acceptable. The key driver behind this is whether it is possible to track and trace the income and expenditure relating to the sub-stream. Section **14.4.3** covers this in more detail, including detail on tracking and tracing.

15.5 Step 3 – allocate debits to sub-streams

Now that the RIPI of each sub-stream has been calculated, the next step is to apportion the debits which are brought into account in calculating the profits of the trade for the accounting period. The debits should be allocated to the standard income stream and the various sub-streams. The debits should be allocated on a just and reasonable basis.

Certain "excluded debits" are not allocated. CTA 2010, s. 357BI sets out the excluded debits, which are:

- debits in respect of loan relationships (CTA 2009, s. 297);
- debits in respect of derivative contracts (CTA 2009, s. 573); and

- the additional deduction relating to R&D tax relief (CTA 2009, Pt. 13), television production relief (Pt. 15A), video games development relief (Pt. 15B), and theatrical production relief (Pt. 15C).

15.6 Step 4 – deduct debits and routine return

The debits allocated under Step 3 are then deducted from the sub-streams along with a routine return.

Certain expenditure which is directly related to income received by the company in respect of a qualifying right is not deducted where it is treated as an "income-related payment". An example could be a licence payment which is directly related to the company's sales of a qualifying item. Further details on this are given at CTA 2010, s. 357BIA.

The routine return aims to remove those profits which a business would have made in the absence of the intellectual property. The routine return is deemed to amount to 10% of specified deductions, which are allocated to the sub-stream at Step 3, as follows:

- capital allowances;
- costs of premises;
- personnel costs;
- plant and machinery costs;
- professional services; and
- various miscellaneous services.

Law: CTA 2010, s. 357BI-357BJB

15.7 Step 5 – deduct the marketing asset return

If the amount calculated under Step 4 for a sub-stream is more than nil then a marketing asset return should be deducted. The marketing asset return is the excess of the "notional marketing royalty" in respect of the sub-stream over the "actual marketing royalty" for that sub-stream. This attempts to prevent returns from marketing assets from benefiting from the reduced tax rate. The legislation provides that the notional marketing royalty should be calculated under transfer pricing principles in line with the OECD *Model Tax Convention* and the OECD *Transfer Pricing Guidelines*. CTA

2010, s. 357BKA sets out the rules for calculating the notional marketing royalty in detail.

For these purposes the relevant marketing assets of a company are:

- anything in respect of which passing off proceedings could be brought, including a registered trademark;
- signs or indications of geographical origin; and
- information relating to customers or potential customers of the company or a group company which is intended for use for marketing purposes.

If the notional marketing royalty, after deducting any actual royalty paid, would be less than 10% of the profits for the sub-stream after deduction of the routine return then the marketing royalty is treated as being nil.

An election can be made for "small claims" which avoids the need to undertake a transfer pricing study. The detailed rules relating to the small claims election are included in CTA 2010, s. 357BN-357BNB.

Law: CTA 2010, s. 357BK-357BKB, 357BN, 357BNB

15.8 Step 6 – the "R&D fraction"

15.8.1 Introduction

The R&D fraction must be applied separately to each sub-stream. The fraction is capped at 1 so that the RIPI cannot be increased. Although several of the definitions of the R&D tax relief are used, there is no requirement to have made an R&D claim.

The R&D fraction is:

$$\frac{(D + S1) * 1.3}{D + S1 + S2 + A}$$

where:

D is the company's expenditure on relevant R&D undertaken in-house;

S1 is the company's qualifying expenditure on relevant R&D subcontracted to unconnected persons;

S2 is the company's qualifying expenditure on relevant R&D subcontracted to connected persons; and

A is the company's expenditure on acquisition of relevant IP rights.

The company must consider the expenditure which relates to the relevant period (see **15.8.2**). The R&D fraction should be reviewed annually to adjust for changes to the inputs.

Expenditure can relate to more than one stream, so an analysis of which sub-stream it relates to must be undertaken. HMRC guidance accepts that this might not be appropriate to allocate the expenditure between streams and an amount could be applied to more than one stream (CIRD 274200).

For accounting periods beginning on or after 1 April 2017, where a company is party to a cost sharing arrangement ("CSA" – see **15.10**), the R&D fraction calculation can be affected by the following:

- R&D undertaken or contracted out by another party to the CSA (CTA 2010, s. 357GCZC);
- acquisition of qualifying IP rights by another party to the CSA (CTA 2010, s. 357GCZD);
- expenditure in connection with the formation of the CSA (CTA 2010, s. 357GCZE); and
- income in connection with the formation of the CSA (CTA 2010, s. 357GCZF)

The methodology for the calculation where the above CSA rules are applied is included in CTA 2010, s. 357BLEA.

Further details on the calculation of the fraction are found at **14.8.**

Law: CTA 2010, s. 357BL, 357BLA, 357BLEA, 357GCZC-GCZF

15.8.2 Relevant period

The period for which you should include expenditure in the R&D fraction is called the relevant period. Reference to the relevant period for the calculation of the R&D fraction is defined by CTA 2010, s. 357BLF. The rules relating to the relevant period are covered in detail at **14.8.7**.

CTA 2010, s. 357BO(2) states that, for the purposes of CTA 2010, s. 357BLF-357BLG, companies claiming under Part 8A, Chapter 2B (old entrant – new IP) are treated as if they are new entrants.

Law: CTA 2010, s. 357BLF-BLG, 357BO

15.9 Step 8 – (if elected for profits before grant) add the profits relating to periods before the grant of the patent.

Where a company makes patent-related profits before the grant of the patent it can elect into the regime to receive benefit from the Patent Box.

To prevent companies from gaining the benefit for products which are not patentable, the benefit of the Patent Box is not received until the patent is granted. When the patent is granted the accumulated patent-related profits for the patent pending period are then included in the calculation for the period of grant. This extension applies to profits in an accounting period where:

- an election for Patent Box relief is in place;
- the company was a qualifying company in that period; and
- the period ends on or after the later of:
    - the first day of the period of six years ending on the grant of the qualifying right, or
    - the date of the filing of the patent application or grant of the exclusive licence.

Where a company is not streaming at the qualifying IP right level it may need to recalculate its R&D fractions to reflect the new IP. In particular, it is important to reconsider the allocation of mixed old/new products and processes (see **15.4.2**).

Law: CTA 2010, s. 357BM

15.10 Cost sharing arrangement ("CSA")

15.10.1 Introduction

If the company is treated as being a party to a CSA where one of the other parties owns qualifying IP then it can also be treated as owning the qualifying IP right.

There are three other facets to the new CSA rules; they can impact:

- the rules regarding new and old IP (see section **11.4**).
- the R&D fraction (see section **15.8**).
- RIPI, as certain income related to the formation of a CSA can be treated as RIPI.

The rules relating to CSAs were rewritten in *Finance (No. 2) Act* 2017. These rules apply for accounting periods beginning on or after 1 April 2017.

The *Explanatory Notes* to F(No. 2)A 2017 state, in relation to the new CSA rules, that:

> "... the result is that the company's own contribution to the development work drives the amount of profit benefiting from the reduced rate."

For accounting periods beginning before 1 April 2017, the CSA rules related only to the ownership requirement. This has been broadly reproduced in the new CSA rules. The key difference between the original CSA definition and the F(No. 2)A 2017 definition is that the requirement that a party to the CSA holds a qualifying IP right or exclusive licence in respect of a qualifying IP right has been removed. The *Explanatory Notes* state that this change was made to recognise that a CSA may, at the outset, have no IP but may intend to develop it.

15.10.2 What is a CSA?

The meaning of a CSA is set out in CTA 2010, s. 357GC, but as noted above care should be taken to ensure that the correct definition is used with the new rules applying for periods beginning on or after 1 April 2017. A CSA under the F(No. 2)A 2017 rules is an arrangement under which all of the following conditions are met:

1. Each party is required to contribute to the cost of, or undertake activities for the purpose of, creating or developing an item or process,
2. Each party:
    - is entitled to a share of the income attributable to the item, or process, or
    - has one or more rights in respect of the item or process; and

3. The amount of any income received is proportionate to its participation in the arrangement in terms of its contribution to the cost or activity (described in Condition 1).

15.11 Application to transferred trades

Where trades are transferred in given circumstances, CTA 2010, s. 357GCA sets out rules that attribute expenditure incurred by the transferor to the transferee. In addition, in certain circumstances, expenditure incurred by the transferee in respect of the assignment, grant or transfer can be ignored for the calculation of the R&D fraction.

Law: CTA 2010, s. 357GCA

Guidance: CIRD 240160, 271100

15.12 Relevant IP losses

It is possible to have relevant IP losses for a given period, which creates a set-off amount which is offset against RIPI of the company or other members of the group. CTA 2010, Pt. 8A, Ch. 5 covers the calculation and offset of these losses in detail.

The possibility that the company could have relevant IP losses should be considered when deciding whether to elect into the Patent Box regime, as the relevant IP losses do not arise if no election is in effect for a period.

Law: CTA 2010, s. 357E-357EF

Appendix 1 – Guidelines on the Meaning of Research and Development for Tax Purposes

These Guidelines are provided by the Department for Business, Innovation and Skills. The Guidelines were issued on 5 March 2004 and updated on 6 December 2010. (Obvious minor errors have been corrected for the purposes of this book.)

These Guidelines are issued by the Secretary of State for Trade and Industry for the purposes of Section 837A Income and Corporation Taxes Act 1988. They replace the previous Guidelines issued on 28 July 2000.

1. Research and development ('R&D') is defined for tax purposes in Section 837A Income and Corporation Taxes Act 1988[1]. This says the definition of R&D for tax purposes follows generally accepted accounting practice. SSAP 13 Accounting for research and development is the Statement of Standard Accounting Practice which defines R&D. The accountancy definition is then modified for tax purposes by these Guidelines, which are given legal force by Parliamentary Regulations. These Guidelines explain what is meant by R&D for a variety of tax purposes, but the rules of particular tax schemes may restrict the qualifying expenditure[2].

2. In these Guidelines a number of terms are used which are intended to have a special meaning for the purpose of the

[1] For the purposes of research and development allowances (Part 6 Capital Allowances Act 2001) this definition is extended to include oil and gas exploration and appraisal as defined in Section 837B Income and Corporation Taxes Act 1988. These Guidelines apply to this extended definition as well.

[2] The original footnotes 2 and 3 to the 2004 Guidelines (which were not themselves part of the Guidelines) have been removed. This is because those footnotes stated that the qualifying indirect activities (QIAs) listed in para 31 are R&D, but do not attract R&D tax credits. In fact, whether or not expenditure on the QIAs qualifies for R&D tax relief depends on a number of factors, but there is no blanket exclusion. For further explanation see, for example, HMRC guidance at http://www.hmrc.gov.uk/manuals/cirdmanual/CIRD83000.htm These revised footnotes are not part of the Guidelines. Revised footnote prepared by Department for Business, Innovation and Skills in consultation with HMRC December 2010.

Guidelines. Such terms are **highlighted** on first appearance and defined later.

The Definition of Research & Development

3. R&D for tax purposes takes place when a **project** seeks to achieve an **advance in science or technology**.

4. The activities which **directly contribute** to achieving this advance in science or technology through the resolution of **scientific or technological uncertainty** are R&D.

5. Certain **qualifying indirect activities** related to the project are also R&D. Activities other than qualifying indirect activities which do not directly contribute to the resolution of the project's scientific or technological uncertainty are not R&D.

Advance in Science or Technology

6. An advance in science or technology means an advance in **overall knowledge or capability** in a field of **science** or technology (not a company's own state of knowledge or capability alone). This includes the adaptation of knowledge or capability from another field of science or technology in order to make such an advance where this adaptation was not readily deducible.

7. An advance in science or technology may have tangible consequences (such as a new or more efficient cleaning product, or a process which generates less waste) or more intangible outcomes (new knowledge or cost improvements, for example).

8. A process, material, device, product, service or source of knowledge does not become an advance in science or technology simply because science or technology is used in its creation. Work which uses science or technology but which does not advance scientific or technological capability as a whole is not an advance in science or technology.

9. A project which seeks to, for example,

    (a) extend overall knowledge or capability in a field of science or technology; or

    (b) create a process, material, device, product or service which incorporates or represents an increase in overall knowledge or capability in a field of science or technology; or

    (c) make an **appreciable improvement** to an existing process, material, device, product or service through scientific or technological changes; or

    (d) use science or technology to duplicate the effect of an existing process, material, device, product or service in a new or appreciably improved way (e.g. a product which has exactly the same performance characteristics as existing models, but is built in a fundamentally different manner)

    will therefore be R&D.

10. Even if the advance in science or technology sought by a project is not achieved or not fully realised, R&D still takes place.

11. If a particular advance in science or technology has already been made or attempted but details are not readily available (for example, if it is a trade secret), work to achieve such an advance can still be an advance in science or technology.

12. However, the routine analysis, copying or adaptation of an existing product, process, service or material, will not be an advance in science or technology.

Scientific or Technological uncertainty

13. Scientific or technological uncertainty exists when knowledge of whether something is scientifically possible or technologically feasible, or how to achieve it in practice, is not readily available or deducible by a competent professional working in the field. This includes **system uncertainty**. Scientific or technological uncertainty will often arise from turning something that has already been established as

scientifically feasible into a cost-effective, reliable and reproducible process, material, device, product or service.

14. Uncertainties that can readily be resolved by a competent professional working in the field are not scientific or technological uncertainties. Similarly, improvements, optimisations and fine-tuning which do not materially affect the underlying science or technology do not constitute work to resolve scientific or technological uncertainty.

Other Definitions

Science

15. Science is the systematic study of the nature and behaviour of the physical and material universe. Work in the arts, humanities and social sciences, including economics, is not science for the purpose of these Guidelines. Mathematical techniques are frequently used in science, but mathematical advances in and of themselves are not science unless they are advances in representing the nature and behaviour of the physical and material universe.

16. These Guidelines apply equally to work in any branch or field of science.

Technology

17. Technology is the practical application of scientific principles and knowledge, where 'scientific' is based on the definition of science above.

18. These Guidelines apply equally to work in any branch or field of technology.

Project

19. A project consists of a number of activities conducted to a method or plan in order to achieve an advance in science or technology. It is important to get the boundaries of the project correct. It should encompass all the activities which collectively serve to resolve the scientific or technological uncertainty associated with achieving the advance, so it could include a number of different sub-projects. A project may

itself be part of a larger commercial project, but that does not make the parts of the commercial project that do not address scientific or technological uncertainty into R&D.

Overall knowledge or capability

20. Overall knowledge or capability in a field of science or technology means the knowledge or capability in the field which is publicly available or is readily deducible from the publicly available knowledge or capability by a competent professional working in the field. Work which seeks an advance relative to this overall knowledge or capability is R&D.

21. Overall knowledge or capability in a field of science or technology can still be advanced (and hence R&D can still be done) in situations where

    - several companies are working at the cutting edge in the same field, and are doing similar work independently; or
    - work has already been done but this is not known in general because it is a trade secret, and another company repeats the work; or
    - it is known that a particular advance in science or technology has been achieved, but the details of how are not readily available.

22. However, the routine analysis, copying or adaptation of an existing process, material, device, product or service will not advance overall knowledge or capability, even though it may be completely new to the company or the company's trade.

Appreciable improvement

23. Appreciable improvement means to change or adapt the scientific or technological characteristics of something to the point where it is 'better' than the original. The improvement should be more than a minor or routine upgrading, and should represent something that would generally be acknowledged by a competent professional working in the field as a genuine and non-trivial improvement.

Improvements arising from the adaptation of knowledge or capability from another field of science or technology are appreciable improvements if they would generally be acknowledged by a competent professional working in the field as a genuine and non-trivial improvement.

24. Improvements which arise from taking existing science or technology and deploying it in a new context (e.g. a different trade) with only minor or routine changes are not appreciable improvements. A process, material, device, product or service will not be appreciably improved if it simply brings a company into line with overall knowledge or capability in science or technology, even though it may be completely new to the company or the company's trade.

25. The question of what scale of advance would constitute an appreciable improvement will differ between fields of science and technology and will depend on what a competent professional working in the field would regard as a genuine and non-trivial improvement.

Directly contribute

26. To directly contribute to achieving an advance in science or technology, an activity (or several activities in combination) must attempt to resolve an element of the scientific or technological uncertainty associated with achieving the advance.

27. Activities which directly contribute to R&D include:

    (a) activities to create or adapt software, materials or equipment needed to resolve the scientific or technological uncertainty, provided that the software, material or equipment is created or adapted solely for use in R&D;

    (b) scientific or technological planning activities; and

    (c) scientific or technological design, testing and analysis undertaken to resolve the scientific or technological uncertainty.

28. Activities which do not directly contribute to the resolution of scientific or technological uncertainty include:

(a) the range of commercial and financial steps necessary for innovation and for the successful development and marketing of a new or appreciably improved process, material, device, product or service;

(b) work to develop non-scientific or non-technological aspects of a new or appreciably improved process, material, device, product or service;

(c) the production and distribution of goods and services;

(d) administration and other supporting services;

(e) general support services (such as transportation, storage, cleaning, repair, maintenance and security); and

(f) qualifying indirect activities.

System uncertainty

29. System uncertainty is scientific or technological uncertainty that results from the complexity of a system rather than uncertainty about how its individual components behave. For example, in electronic devices, the characteristics of individual components or chips are fixed, but there can still be uncertainty about the best way to combine those components to achieve an overall effect. However, assembling a number of components (or software sub-programs) to an established pattern, or following routine methods for doing so, involves little or no scientific or technological uncertainty.

30. Similarly, work on combining standard technologies, devices, and/or processes can involve scientific or technological uncertainty even if the principles for their integration are well known. There will be scientific or technological uncertainty if a competent professional working in the field cannot readily deduce how the separate components or sub-systems should be combined to have the intended function.

Qualifying indirect activity

31. These are activities which form part of a project but do not directly contribute to the resolution of the scientific or technological uncertainty. They are:

    (a) scientific and technical information services, insofar as they are conducted for the purpose of R&D support (such as the preparation of the original report of R&D findings);

    (b) indirect supporting activities such as maintenance, security, administration and clerical activities, and finance and personnel activities, insofar as undertaken for R&D;

    (c) ancillary activities essential to the undertaking of R&D (e.g. taking on and paying staff, leasing laboratories and maintaining research and development equipment including computers used for R&D purposes);

    (d) training required to directly support an R&D project;

    (e) research by students and researchers carried out at universities;

    (f) research (including related data collection) to devise new scientific or technological testing, survey, or sampling methods, where this research is not R&D in its own right; and

    (g) feasibility studies to inform the strategic direction of a specific R&D activity.

32. Activities not described in paragraph 31 are not qualifying indirect activities.

Commentary on particular questions which arise

Start and end of R&D

33. R&D begins when work to resolve the scientific or technological uncertainty starts, and ends when that uncertainty is resolved or work to resolve it ceases. This means that work to identify the requirements for the process,

material, device, product or service, where no scientific or technological questions are at issue, is not R&D.

34. R&D ends when knowledge is codified in a form usable by a competent professional working in the field, or when a prototype or pilot plant with all the functional characteristics of the final process, material, device, product or service is produced.

35. Although the R&D for a process, material, device, product or service may have ended, new problems which involve scientific or technological uncertainty may emerge after it has been turned over to production or put into use. The resolution of these problems may require new R&D to be carried out. But there is a distinction to be drawn between such problems and routine fault fixing.

Planning as part of R&D

36. Scientific or technological planning activities associated with a project directly contribute to resolving the scientific or technological uncertainty associated with the project, and are therefore R&D. These include defining scientific or technological objectives, assessing scientific or technological feasibility, identifying particular scientific or technological uncertainties, estimating development time, schedule, and resources of the R&D, and high-level outlining of the scientific or technical work, as well as the detailed planning and management of the work.

37. Elements of a company's planning activity relating to a project but not directly contributing to the resolution of scientific or technological uncertainty, such as identifying or researching market niches in which R&D might benefit a company, or examination of a project's financial, marketing, and legal aspects, fall outside the category of scientific or technological planning, and are therefore not R&D

Abortive projects

38. Not all projects succeed in their aims. What counts is whether there is an intention to achieve an advance in science or technology, not whether ultimately the associated scientific or

technological uncertainty is completely resolved, or resolved to the degree intended. Scientific or technological planning activities associated with projects which are not taken forward (e.g. because of insurmountable technical or commercial challenges) are still R&D.

Prototypes, pilot plants

39. A prototype is an original model on which something new or appreciably improved is patterned, and of which all things of the same type are representations or copies. It is a basic experimental model possessing the essential characteristics of the intended process, material, device, product or service. The design, construction, and testing of prototypes generally fall within the scope of R&D for tax purposes. But once any modifications necessary to reflect the test findings have been made to the prototypes, and further testing has been satisfactorily completed, the scientific or technological uncertainty has been resolved and further work will not be R&D.

40. Similarly the construction and operation of pilot plants while assessing their operations is R&D until the scientific or technological uncertainty associated with the intended advance in science or technology has been resolved.

Design

41. When achieving design objectives requires the resolution of scientific or technological uncertainty within a project, work to do this will be R&D. Design activities which do not directly contribute to the resolution of scientific or technological uncertainty within a project are not R&D.

Cosmetic and aesthetic effects

42. Cosmetic and aesthetic qualities are not of themselves science or technology, and so work to improve the cosmetic or aesthetic appeal of a process, material, device, product or service would not in itself be R&D. However, work to create a desired cosmetic or aesthetic effect through the application of science or technology can require a scientific or technological

advance, and resolving the scientific or technological uncertainty associated with such a project would therefore be R&D.

Content delivered through science or technology

43. Information or other content which is delivered through a scientific or technological medium is not of itself science or technology. However, improvements in scientific or technological means to create, manipulate and transfer information or other content can be scientific or technological advances, and resolving the scientific or technological uncertainty associated with such projects would therefore be R&D.

Examples / Illustrations

Examples in these Guidelines are illustrative, designed to cast light on the principles explained in the Guidelines, and should be read in that context.

A. The R&D process

A1. A company conducts extensive market research to learn what technical and design characteristics a new DVD player should have in order to be an appealing product. This work is not R&D (paragraph 37). However, it does identify a potential project to create a DVD player incorporating a number of technological improvements which the company's R&D staff (who are competent professionals) regard as genuine and nontrivial. This project would be seeking to develop an appreciably improved DVD player (paragraphs 23-25) and would therefore be seeking to achieve an advance in science or technology (paragraph 9(c)).

A2. The company then decides on a detailed specification for the desired new product, and devises a plan for developing it. Some elements of this plan involve planning of activities which directly contribute to resolving the project's scientific or technological uncertainties (such as the system uncertainty associated with an improved control mechanism for the laser that 'reads' the DVD). This element of planning is R&D (paragraph 36), as are the activities themselves (paragraph 4). Other elements of the plan focus on obtaining intellectual property protection or cosmetic design decisions, for example, which do not directly contribute to resolving the project's scientific or technological uncertainties and are not qualifying indirect activities (paragraph 31) and are therefore not R&D. Neither this planning (paragraph 37) nor these activities (paragraph 28) are R&D.

A3. The scientific or technological work culminates in the creation of a series of prototype DVD players, and ultimately a 'final' prototype is produced and tested which possesses the essential characteristics of the intended product (circuit board design, performance characteristics, etc.). All the activities which directly contributed to resolving the scientific or technological uncertainty of creating the DVD player up to this point (such as the testing of successive prototypes) are R&D (paragraphs 34 and 39).

A4. Several copies of this prototype are made (not R&D; paragraphs 4-5 and 26-28) and distributed to a group of consumers to test their reactions (not R&D; paragraph 28((a)). Some of these consumers report concerns about the noise level of the DVD player in operation. Additional work is done to resolve this problem. If this involves a routine adjustment of the existing prototype (i.e. no scientific or technological uncertainty) then it will not be R&D (paragraph 14); if it involves more substantial changes (i.e. there is scientific or technological uncertainty to resolve) then it will be R&D.

B. Equal applicability in any branch or field of science or technology

B1. The Guidelines apply equally to work in any branch or field of science or technology (paragraphs 15-18). This means that work in software engineering, for example, is subject to the same fundamental criteria for being R&D as work in textile science, or nanotechnology, or anything else.

B2. This equality also applies to the methods used to resolve scientific or technological uncertainty. For example, it is sometimes possible to implement functionality in a product or process by means of software or of hardware. As long as the scientific or technological uncertainty cannot readily be resolved by a competent professional working in the field, hardware and software methods are both equally R&D in these circumstances.

C. Abortive projects

C1. Not all projects achieve the advance in science or technology they are seeking. For example, work to insert a particular gene into a gene sequence may simply fail, while an attempt to appreciably increase the life of a battery may only yield a marginal improvement. In both cases, the project seeks to achieve an advance in science or technology and work to resolve the scientific or technological uncertainty would be R&D (paragraph 10).

D. Advance in science or technology

D1. Searching for the molecular structures of possible new drugs would be an advance in science or technology, because it applies existing knowledge of science (which compounds are known to cause particular physiological effects) in search of new or improved active compounds (paragraph 9(b)). This is true even if the method used to search for those molecular structures (e.g. running a computer programme on a particular set of data) is itself entirely routine; the activity directly contributes to the resolution of scientific or technological uncertainty (paragraph 27(c)) and so would be R&D (paragraph 4) . Work to identify new uses of existing compounds would also be creative work in science or technology, because it seeks new scientific knowledge about those molecules (paragraph 9(a)).

D2. However, the development of software intended for the analysis of market research data (which is not scientific or technological knowledge; paragraphs 15-18) which was not expected to result in the development of a scientific or technological advance in the field of software as a whole (such as an algorithm which extends overall knowledge or capability in the field of software) would not be R&D (paragraph 8). Work to adapt such software to analyse, say, customer spending patterns would also not be R&D.

D3. An advance in science or technology need not imply an absolute improvement in the performance of a process, material, device, product or service. For example, the existence of high-fidelity audio equipment does not prevent a project to create lower-performance equipment from being an advance in science or technology (for instance, if it incorporated technological improvements leading to lower cost through more efficient circuit design or speaker construction) (paragraph 9(d)).

E. Scientific or technological uncertainty

E1. A firm's project involves finding a new active ingredient for weed-killer (an advance in overall knowledge or capability in the particular field of science or technology; paragraphs 6, 20), and developing a formula incorporating the new active ingredient for use in a commercial product (paragraph 9(b) or (c)). Both of these would constitute an advance in science or technology.

E2. In order to achieve this advance, a programme of investigation by computer to pick likely ingredients and the systematic testing of possible ingredients and products based on those 'trial' ingredients is undertaken. The work involves the adaptation of existing software to tackle the specific problem, and product formulation and testing using established methods. This investigation and testing evaluates the weed-killing performance and other relevant characteristics of the formulations (for example, toxicity to humans and wildlife, water solubility, adhesion to weeds, damage done to other plants). All of these activities would therefore be R&D (paragraphs 4, 26, 27).

E3. The company also does work to assess what characteristics a new weed-killing product should have in order to appeal to consumers. This activity does not directly contribute to the resolution of scientific or technological uncertainty (paragraph 28(a)) and is not a qualifying indirect activity (paragraph 31), and is therefore not R&D (paragraph 4).

F. Direct contribution to the resolution of scientific or technological uncertainty

F1. Work to compare the effectiveness of two possible designs for controlling part of a new manufacturing process would directly contribute to resolving the scientific or technological uncertainty inherent in the new process, and hence the activity would be R&D (paragraphs 4,26). But work to raise finance for the project, while indirectly contributing to the resolution of scientific or technological uncertainty (e.g. by paying for work) does not of itself help resolve the uncertainty, and hence is not R&D (paragraph 28(a)). Human Resources work to support the R&D is a qualifying indirect activity (paragraph 31) and hence is also R&D (paragraph 5), though it does not directly contribute to the resolution of scientific or technological uncertainty (paragraph 28(e) and (f))[3].

G. Testing as part of R&D

G1. Scientific or technological testing and analysis which directly contributes to the resolution of scientific or technological uncertainty is R&D (paragraph 26). So for example if testing work is carried out as part of the development of a pilot plant, this would be R&D, but once the design of the 'final' pilot plant had been finalised and tested, any further testing would not be R&D (paragraph 39). However, if flaws in the design became apparent later on, then work to remedy them would be R&D if they could not readily be resolved by a competent professional working in the field (in other words, if there was scientific or technological uncertainty around how to fix the problem; paragraph 14).

H. Cosmetic and aesthetic effects

H1. A company is seeking to make a water-breathable fabric for use in hiking gear. A test fabric with the required physical characteristics is produced through R&D. This new fabric is then produced in small quantities (not R&D) and market tested with a number of trial users. The user tests are not R&D, because they are concerned with testing the commercial potential of the new material and assessing its appeal to users (paragraph 42).

H2. One of the results of these tests is that users do not like the feel of the new fabric against their skin, and dislike its shiny appearance. The company decides to investigate variants of its new fabric, which require significant changes to the material's weave and physical structure, to overcome these problems. Because there is scientific and technological uncertainty around whether a material with the desired physical characteristics can be made, the R&D continues.

[3] See footnote 2.

J. Project, prototype and end of R&D

J1. A company develops new spark plugs for use in an existing petrol engine. The scientific or technological uncertainty associated with this work is resolved once prototype plugs have been fully tested in the engine. The activities directly contributing to this work, including the construction of prototypes and their testing in the engine, would be R&D.

J2. The same company decides to design a new engine to incorporate the new spark plugs, involving a new combustion chamber design, lighter materials and other improvements such that the overall engine is appreciably improved (it uses less petrol to achieve slightly greater power output performance, and generates less pollution than current models). The activities directly contributing to this work, including the design of the separate components (not all of which need be different from those used in previous models) and their integration into a new engine, are R&D. The uncertainty associated with this work is resolved, and R&D is complete once a functionally final prototype has been tested.

Appendix 2 – Definition of SME: EU Commission Recommendation

Commission Recommendation (2003/361/EC)

of 6 May 2003 concerning the definition of micro, small and medium-sized enterprises

The Commission of the European Communities,

Having regard to the Treaty establishing the European Community, and in particular Article 211, second indent, thereof,

Whereas:

(1) In a report submitted to the Council in 1992 at the request of the 'Industry' Council held on 28 May 1990, the Commission had proposed limiting the proliferation of definitions of small and medium-sized enterprises in use at Community level. Commission Recommendation 96/280/EC of 3 April 1996 concerning the definition of small and medium-sized enterprises[1] was based on the idea that the existence of different definitions at Community level and at national level could create inconsistencies. Following the logic of a single market without internal frontiers, the treatment of enterprises should be based on a set of common rules. The pursuit of such an approach is all the more necessary in view of the extensive interaction between national and Community measures assisting micro, small and medium-sized enterprises (SME), for example in connection with Structural Funds or research. It means that situations in which the Community focuses its action on a given category of SMEs and the Member States on another must be avoided. In addition, it was considered that the application of the same definition by the Commission, the Member States, the European Investment Bank (EIB) and the European Investment Fund (EIF) would improve the consistency and effectiveness of policies

[1] OJ L 107, 30.4.1996, p. 4

targeting SMEs and would, therefore, limit the risk of distortion of competition.

(2) Recommendation 96/280/EC has been applied widely by the Member States, and the definition contained in the Annex thereto has been taken over in Commission Regulation (EC) No 70/2001 of 12 January 2001 on the application of Articles 87 and 88 of the EC Treaty to State aid to small and medium-sized enterprises[2]. Apart from the need to adapt Recommendation 96/280/EC to economic developments, pursuant to Article 2 of the Annex thereto, consideration must be given to a number of difficulties of interpretation which have emerged in its application, as well as the observations received from enterprises. In view of the number of amendments now requiring to be made to Recommendation 96/280/EC, and for the sake of clarity, it is appropriate to replace the Recommendation.

(3) It should also be made clear what, in accordance with Articles 48, 81 and 82 of the Treaty, as interpreted by the Court of Justice of the European Communities, an enterprise should be considered to be any entity, regardless of its legal form, engaged in economic activities, including in particular entities engaged in a craft activity and other activities on an individual or family basis, partnerships or associations regularly engaged in economic activities.

(4) The criterion of staff numbers (the 'staff headcount criterion') remains undoubtedly one of the most important, and must be observed as the main criterion; introducing a financial criterion is nonetheless a necessary adjunct in order to grasp the real scale and performance of an enterprise and its position compared to its competitors. However, it would not be desirable to use turnover as the sole financial criterion, in particular because enterprises in the trade and distribution sector have by their nature higher turnover figures than those in the manufacturing sector. Thus the turnover criterion should be combined with that of the balance sheet total, a

[2] OJ L 10, 13.1.2001, p. 33.

criterion which reflects the overall wealth of a business, with the possibility of either of these two criteria being exceeded.

(5) The turnover ceiling refers to enterprises engaged in very different types of economic activity. In order not to restrict unduly the usefulness of applying the definition, it should be updated to take account of changes in both prices and productivity.

(6) As regards the ceiling for the balance sheet total, in the absence of any new element, it is justified to maintain the approach whereby the turnover ceilings are subjected to a coefficient based on the statistical ratio between the two variables. The statistical trend requires a greater increase to be made to the turnover ceiling. Since the trend differs according to the size-category of the enterprise, it is also appropriate to adjust the coefficient in order to reflect the economic trend as closely as possible and not to penalise micro enterprises and small enterprises as opposed to medium-sized enterprises. This coefficient is very close to 1 in the case of micro enterprises and small enterprises. To simplify matters, therefore, a single value must be chosen for those categories for the turnover ceiling and balance sheet total ceiling.

(7) As in Recommendation 96/280/EC, the financial ceilings and the staff ceilings represent maximum limits and the Member States, the EIB and the EIF may fix ceilings lower than the Community ceilings if they wish to direct their measures towards a specific category of SME. In the interests of administrative simplification, the Member States, the EIB and the EIF may use only one criterion – the staff headcount – for the implementation of some of their policies. However, this does not apply to the various rules in competition law where the financial criteria must also be used and adhered to.

(8) Following the endorsement of the European Charter for Small Enterprises by the European Council of Santa Maria da Feira in June 2000, micro enterprises – a category of small enterprises particularly important for the development of entrepreneurship and job creation – should also be better defined.

(9) To gain a better understanding of the real economic position of SMEs and to remove from that category groups of enterprises whose economic power may exceed that of genuine SMEs, a distinction should be made between various types of enterprises, depending on whether they are autonomous, whether they have holdings which do not entail a controlling position (partner enterprises), or whether they are linked to other enterprises. The current limit shown in Recommendation 96/280/EC, of a 25% holding below which an enterprise is considered autonomous, is maintained.

(10) In order to encourage the creation of enterprises, equity financing of SMEs and rural and local development, enterprises can be considered autonomous despite a holding of 25% or more by certain categories of investors who have a positive role in business financing and creation. However, conditions for these investors have not previously been specified. The case of 'business angels' (individuals or groups of individuals pursuing a regular business of investing venture capital) deserves special mention because – compared to other venture capital investors – their ability to give relevant advice to new entrepreneurs is extremely valuable. Their investment in equity capital also complements the activity of venture capital companies, as they provide smaller amounts at an earlier stage of the enterprise's life.

(11) To simplify matters, in particular for Member States and enterprises, use should be made when defining linked enterprises of the conditions laid down in Article 1 of Council Directive 83/349/EEC of 13 June 1983 based on Article 54(3)(g) of the Treaty on consolidated accounts[3], as last amended b) Directive 2001/65/EC of the European Parliament and of the Council[4], in so far as these conditions are suitable for the purposes of this Recommendation. To strengthen the incentives for investing in the equity funding of an SME, the presumption of absence of dominant influence on the enterprise in question was introduced, in pursuance of

[3] OJ L 193, 18.7.1983, p. 1
[4] OJ L 283, 27.10.2001, p. 28

the criteria of Article 5(3), of Council Directive 78/660/EEC of 25 July 1978 based on Article 54(5)(g) of the Treaty on the annual accounts of certain types of companies[5], as last amended by Directive 2001/65/EC.

(12) Account should also be taken, in suitable cases, of relations between enterprises, which pass through natural persons, with a view to ensuring that only those enterprises which really need the advantages accruing to SMEs from the different rules or measures in their favour actually benefit from them. In order to limit the examination of these situations to the strict minimum, the account taken of such relationships has been restricted to the relevant market or to adjacent markets – reference being had, where necessary, to the Commission's definition of 'relevant markets' in the Commission notice on the definition of relevant market for the purposes of Community competition law [6].

(13) In order to avoid arbitrary distinctions between different public bodies of a Member State, and given the need for legal certainty, it is considered necessary to confirm that an enterprise with 25% or more of its capital or voting rights controlled by a public body is not an SME.

(14) In order to ease the administrative burden for enterprises, and to simplify and speed up the administrative handling of cases for which SME status is required, it is appropriate to allow enterprises to use solemn declarations to certify certain of their characteristics.

(15) It is necessary to establish in detail the composition of the staff headcount for SME definition purposes. In order to promote the development of vocational training and sandwich courses, it is desirable, when calculating staff numbers, to disregard apprentices and students with a vocational training contract. Similarly, maternity or parental leave periods should not be counted.

5 OJ L 222, 14.8.1978, p. 11
6 OJ C 372, 9.12.1997, p. 5

(16) The various types of enterprise defined according to their relationship with other enterprises correspond to objectively differing degrees of integration. It is therefore appropriate to apply distinct procedures to each of those types of enterprise when calculating the quantities representing their activities and economic power.

Hereby Recommends:

Article 1

1. This Recommendation concerns the definition of micro, small and medium-sized enterprises used in Community policies applied within the Community and the European Economic Area.

2. Member States, the European Investment Bank (EIB) and the European Investment Fund (EIF), are invited:

   (a) to comply with Title I of the Annex for their programmes directed towards medium-sized enterprises, small enterprises or micro enterprises;

   (b) to take the necessary steps with a view to using the size classes set out in Article 7 of the Annex, especially where the monitoring of their use of Community financial instruments is concerned.

Article 2

The ceilings shown in Article 2 of the Annex are to be regarded as maximum values. Member States, the EIB and the EIF may fix lower ceilings. In implementing certain of their policies, they may also choose to apply only the criterion of number of employees, except in fields governed by the various rules on State aid.

Article 3

This Recommendation will replace Recommendation 96/280/EC as from 1 January 2005.

Article 4

This Recommendation is addressed to the Member States, the EIB and the EIF.

They are requested to inform the Commission by 31 December 2004 of any measures they have taken further to it and, no later than 30 September 2005, to inform it of the first results of its implementation.

Done at Brussels, 6 May 2003.

For the Commission

Erkki LIIKANEN

Member of the Commission

Annex

Title I

Definition of micro, small and medium-sized enterprises adopted by the Commission

Article I

Enterprise

An enterprise is considered to be any entity engaged in an economic activity, irrespective of its legal form. This includes, in particular, self-employed persons and family businesses engaged in craft or other activities, and partnerships or associations regularly engaged in an economic activity.

Article 2

Staff headcount and financial ceilings determining enterprise categories

1. The category of micro, small and medium-sized enterprises (SMEs) is made up of enterprises which employ fewer than 250 persons and which have an annual turnover not exceeding €50 million, and/or an annual balance sheet total not exceeding €43 million.

2. Within the SME category, a small enterprise is defined as an enterprise which employs fewer than 50; persons and whose annual turnover and/or annual balance sheet total does not exceed €10 million.

3. Within the SME category, a micro enterprise is defined as an enterprise which employs fewer than 10 persons and whose annual turnover and/or annual balance sheet total does not exceed €2 million.

Article 3

Types of enterprise taken into consideration in calculating staff numbers and financial amounts

1. An 'autonomous enterprise' is any enterprise which is not classified as a partner enterprise within the meaning of paragraph 2 or as a linked enterprise within the meaning of paragraph 3.

2. 'Partner enterprises' are all enterprises which are not classified as linked enterprises within the meaning of paragraph 3 and between which there is the following relationship: an enterprise (upstream enterprise) holds, either solely or jointly with one or more linked enterprises within the meaning of paragraph 3, 25% or more of the capital or voting rights of another enterprise (downstream enterprise).

   However, an enterprise may be ranked as autonomous, and thus as not having any partner enterprises, even if this 25% threshold is reached or exceeded by the following investors, provided that those investors are not linked, within the meaning of paragraph 3, either individually or jointly to the enterprise in question:

   (a) public investment corporations, venture capital companies, individuals or groups of individuals with a regular venture capital investment activity who invest equity capital in unquoted businesses ('business angels') provided the total investment of those business angels in the same enterprise is less than €1 250 000;

(b) universities or non-profit research centres;

(c) institutional investors, including regional development funds;

(d) autonomous local authorities with an annual budget of less than €10 million and fewer than 5 000 inhabitants.

3. 'Linked enterprises' are enterprises which have any of the following relationships with each other:

(a) an enterprise has a majority of the shareholders' or members' voting rights in another enterprise;

(b) an enterprise has the right to appoint or remove a majority of the members of the administrative, management or supervisory body of another enterprise;

(c) an enterprise has the right to exercise a dominant influence over another enterprise pursuant to a contract entered into with that enterprise or to a provision in its memorandum or articles of association;

(d) an enterprise, which is a shareholder in or member of another enterprise, controls alone, pursuant to an agreement with other shareholders in or members of that enterprise, a majority of shareholders or members' voting rights in that enterprise.

There is a presumption that no dominant influence exists if the investors listed in the second subparagraph of paragraph 2 are not involving themselves directly or indirectly in the management of the enterprise in question, without prejudice to their rights as stakeholders.

Enterprises having any of the relationships described in the first subparagraph through one or more other enterprises, or any one of the investors mentioned in paragraph 2, are also considered to be linked.

Enterprises which have one or other of such relationships through a natural person or group of natural persons acting jointly are also considered linked enterprises if they engage in their activity or in part of their activity in the same relevant market or in adjacent markets.

An 'adjacent market' is considered to be the market for a product or service situated directly upstream or downstream of the relevant market.

4. Except in the cases set out in paragraph 2, second subparagraph, an enterprise cannot be considered an SME if 25% or more of the capital or voting rights are directly or indirectly controlled, jointly or individually, by one or more public bodies.

5. Enterprises may make a declaration of status as an autonomous enterprise, partner enterprise or linked enterprise, including the data regarding the ceilings set out in Article 2. The declaration may be made even if the capital is spread in such a way that it is not possible to determine exactly by whom it is held, in which case the enterprise may declare in good faith that it can legitimately presume that it is not owned as to 25% or more by one enterprise or jointly by enterprises linked to one another. Such declarations are made without prejudice to the checks and investigations provided for by national or Community rules.

Article 4

Data used for the staff headcount and the financial amounts and reference period

1. The data to apply to the headcount of staff and the financial amounts are those relating to the latest approved accounting period and calculated on an annual basis. They are taken into account from the date of closure of the accounts. The amount selected for the turnover is calculated excluding value-added tax (VAT) and other indirect taxes.

2. Where, at the date of closure of the accounts, an enterprise finds that, on an annual basis, it has exceeded or fallen below the headcount or financial ceilings stated in Article 2, this will

not result in the loss or acquisition of the status of medium-sized, small or micro enterprise unless those ceilings are exceeded over two consecutive accounting periods.

3. In the case of newly established enterprises whose accounts have not yet been approved, the data to apply is to be derived from a bona fide estimate made in the course of the financial year.

Article 5

Staff headcount

The headcount corresponds to the number of annual work units (AWU), i.e. the number of persons who worked full-time within the enterprise in question or on its behalf during the entire reference year under consideration, the work of persons who have not worked the full year, the work of those who have worked part-time, regardless of duration, and the work of seasonal workers are counted as fractions of AWU. The staff consists of:

(a) employees;

(b) persons working for the enterprise being subordinated to it and deemed to be employees under national law;

(c) owner-manager;

(d) partners engaging in a regular activity in the enterprise and benefiting from financial advantages from the enterprise.

Apprentices or students engaged in vocational training with an apprenticeship or vocational training contract are not included as staff. The duration of maternity or parental leaves is not counted.

Article 6

Establishing the data of an enterprise

1. In the case of an autonomous enterprise, the data, including the number of staff, are determined exclusively on the basis of the accounts of that enterprise.

2. The data, including the headcount, of an enterprise having partner enterprises or linked enterprises are determined on the basis of the accounts and other data of the enterprise or, where they exist, the consolidated accounts of the enterprise, or the consolidated accounts in which the enterprise is included through consolidation.

   To the data referred to in the first subparagraph are added the data of any partner enterprise of the enterprise in question situated immediately upstream or downstream from it. Aggregation is proportional to the percentage interest in the capital or voting rights (whichever is greater). In the case of cross-holdings, the greater percentage applies.

   To the data referred to in the first and second subparagraph is added 100% of the data of any enterprise, which is linked directly or indirectly to the enterprise in question, where the data were not already included through consolidation in the accounts.

3. For the application of paragraph 2, the data of the partner enterprises of the enterprise in question are derived from their accounts and their other data, consolidated if they exist. To these is added 100% of the data of enterprises, which are linked to these partner enterprises, unless their accounts data are already included through consolidation.

4. For the application of the same paragraph 2, the data of the enterprises, which are linked to the enterprise in question, are to be derived from their accounts and their other data, consolidated if they exist. To these is added, pro rata, the data of any possible partner enterprise of that linked enterprise, situated immediately upstream or downstream from it, unless it has already been included in the consolidated accounts with a percentage at least proportional to the percentage identified under the second subparagraph of paragraph 2.

5. Where in the consolidated accounts no staff data appear for a given enterprise, staff figures are calculated by aggregating proportionally the data from its partner enterprises and by adding the data from the enterprises to which the enterprise in question is linked.

Title II

Sundry provisions

Article 7

Statistics

The Commission will take the necessary measures to present the statistics that it produces in accordance with the following size-classes of enterprises:

(a) 0 to 1 person;

(b) 2 to 9 persons;

(c) 10 to 49 persons;

(d) 50 to 249 persons.

Article 8

References

1. Any Community legislation or any Community programme to be amended or adopted and in which the term 'SME', 'micro enterprise', 'small enterprise' or 'medium-sized enterprise', or any other similar term occurs, should refer to the definition contained in this Recommendation.

2. As a transitional measure, current Community programmes using the SME definition in Recommendation 96/280/EC will continue to be implemented for the benefit of the enterprises, which were considered SMEs when those programmes were adopted. Legally binding commitments entered into by the Commission on the basis of such programmes will remain unaffected.

   Without prejudice to the first subparagraph, any amendment of the SME definition within the programme can be made only by adopting the definition contained in this Recommendation in accordance with paragraph 1.

Article 9

Revision

On the basis of a review of the application of the definition contained in this Recommendation, to be drawn up by 31 March 2006, and taking account of any amendments to Article 1 of Directive 83/349/EEC on the definition of linked enterprises within the meaning of that Directive, the Commission will, if necessary, adapt the definition contained in this Recommendation, and in particular the ceilings for turnover and the balance-sheet total in order to take account of experience and economic developments in the Community.

Table of legislation

Capital Allowances Act 2001

Companies Act 2006

Corporation Tax Act 2009

Corporation Tax Act 2010

Index of cases

General index

Printed and bound in Great Britain by
Marston Book Services Limited, Oxfordshire